MODERN TECHNIQUES FOR AUTO RESTORATION

KEN WICKHAM

Published by

**krause
publications**

700 E. State Street • Iola, WI 54990-0001
Telephone: 715/445-2214

Please call or write for our free catalog.
Our toll-free number to place an order or obtain a free catalog is 800-258-0929
or please use our regular business telephone 715-445-2214
for editorial comment and further information.

Library of Congress Catalog Number: 97-80605
ISBN: 0-87341-571-X

Printed in the United States of America

My theory is to restore the car so that it will last at least 20 years in prime condition. Obviously, you do not drive a show car every day and this counts for many of those years, but the quality of the restoration is crucial.

– **Ken Wickham**

Table of Contents

Foreword

After writing this book, I found myself a quiet place and sat down for my first reading. I mentally traveled back in time, back to the point in my life when I decided to buy my first classic automobile. I asked myself, "What do I wish I knew then that I know now?", and, "What, if anything, have I left out of this book?"

The answer to the first question is what this book is all about. I made a lot of mistakes when restoring my first automobile. I have come to realize that the most important steps in a successful auto restoration *are not found in the actual restoration of the car, but in the planning stages beforehand.*

I also write a restoration column and conduct restoration seminars for the Pontiac Oakland Club International. My interaction with the club membership has given me a great advantage. I save every letter I receive and write down every question asked of me in my seminars. I have organized all of this material into a journal.

The most common questions asked of me are related to government involvement in the restoration hobby, safety and confidence ("Can I do it?"). The answer to the confidence question is *"Yes, you can do it."* Restoration is not that difficult, but it does take a great deal of patience. Most people spend years restoring a car. It also takes money. The amount of money spent mainly depends on the type of restoration performed (there's that planning thing, again). Restoring a car strictly for show can be expensive. The chrome plating alone for show cars can cost as much as $10,000. This price has increased dramatically over the past couple of years. In fact, many costs associated with auto restoration have increased in this same time period. This is due, mainly, to a series of new environmental laws and increased government regulation.

As I scan through the letters I receive, I have noticed a trend. There seems to be a growing resentment towards government involvement in our hobby. I must confess that I, too, resent this intrusion and you will detect this attitude within the pages of this book. I apologize in advance to those of you who may be offended by my attitude, but after witnessing firsthand much of the craziness that takes place in the name of environmentalism I will defend my attitude to any and all. I also believe that "attitude" is what separates this restoration book from all the rest.

And it's not that I think all government is bad, as government involvement has created some positive measures. The most important of these measures has been the heightened awareness of safety.

I am considered by most to be a young hobbyist. However, when I look around, I do not see a lot of older people painting cars. Naturally, I have to ask why? What I discovered is somewhat disturbing. Due to the lack of proper safety equipment, many people involved in the painting/restoration industries up through the 1980s have had health complications. Without getting too gruesome, many of the restoration products and paints contain chemicals that can cause serious damage to your liver and central nervous system. Always work in a well-ventilated area and wear an approved respirator when using these products. All of these products have safety directions on their container labels, many of which were mandated by our government. Please take the time to read these directions and follow the advice given.

Ken Wickham

Introduction

How It Begins

An auto restoration always begins with a dream. The dream might be conquering or overcoming an obstacle. Maybe it's that we want to cruise through town in a beautiful classic or just to enjoy our memories of the past. It would be great to finally get the car we always wanted, but could not afford, when we were younger. Perhaps, it's even the car that dad owned when you learned to drive. The list of dreams is endless...

You've been dreaming about owning a muscle car since the ninth grade, but now you have the financial resources to make that dream come true. (1967 Pontiac GTO)

Wouldn't it be nice to have Dad's old car again? (1955 Buick Century convertible)

Then you finally stop talking about it, and just do it. You purchase a pile of junk that resembles a car. Of course this decision seems to be "spur of the moment" to those around you, but you've been contemplating this for years.

This is how I got my start in restoring automobiles. I wanted to be seen. I wanted to cruise through town, and be the only one with a particular kind of car. I wanted to be different. It's rather hard these days to express individuality when most cars basically look the same.

So there it was, abandoned on the side of the road. It seemed so pitiful, rusting away in the weeds. I didn't even know what kind of car it was and certainly knew absolutely nothing about how to restore it, but I was excited and bought the car anyway. I finally learned what model the car was when I received the title six weeks later! Of course, I had no restoration skills nor any idea how much time and money would be needed to complete a project such as this. I completely underestimated the task ahead of me. It's the lack of this information in the beginning that usually leads to the failure of a restoration project in the end. I cannot tell you how many times people call me asking for restoration information and end up not liking what they hear. I explain to

All the cars seem to look the same now. Is there any wonder why there has been such an interest in classic automobiles?

them that a restoration can take a year or more and cost thousands of dollars. Keep in mind that when you pay someone by the hour to do everything for you that the cost escalates quickly. The person on the phone usually counters with information about some other shop that will do a frame off restoration in 90 days and it will only cost $20,000 because the shop has 30 employees. Use common sense. Think about the overhead of such a facility. How many cars per month would have to go through it to meet that overhead? It usually takes twice that long alone to get the chrome plating done. Is this facility charging by the hour? What assurance do you have that you won't eventually hear: "Oops, we weren't expecting that much rust. This is going to take a lot longer than we thought." Or is this facility's owner just telling you what you want to hear to get you in the door?

I did not have that kind of money for my restoration project, so I decided to restore this car myself. Three years later, I had the drivetrain rebuilt and an amateur paint job applied. All I really lacked was some interior and stainless trim work. At this point, I left home to visit my family for Christmas, and that's when my whole life changed. The nearly finished car had been safely parked behind our house for years, but the moment I left town the area received an extended rainfall of biblical proportions. A nearby lake (66 miles long, by the way) rose 22 feet in one week. We've never had rain like that! I returned to find my dream four feet under water. To make matters worse, our house was full of gas and oil (it definitely floats)! That was one of the harshest moments of my life.

This was the actual car as found in northern Oklahoma. Even though the area was mowed and well kept, the grass growing through the car was several feet high. You think that the owner mowed around the car to help sell it? You think the car might have been sitting there a long time? I should have noticed that and offered less. Oh well!

I had spent $10,000 for a feeling of total despair. I started to recall the time when my neighbor stopped by and laughed at my dream. Then there was the time my friend told me to quit immediately before I wasted any more time. I still remember the jokes, and certainly remember all of the chuckles. All I could do was ask: 'What did I do wrong and why was I being punished this way'? Of course, I now look back on this tragedy with a different attitude. I didn't know it at the time, but the flood was actually a blessing.

In the meantime, I began working part-time in a professional restoration shop. I found the work interesting, and the extra cash helped me pay the bills while I was in college. This shop mainly restored 1957 Chevys, but working there taught me to pay attention to detail if you wanted to win at the shows. The '57 Chevrolet is not particularly difficult to restore, but it is judged in one of the most difficult classes to win at shows. You might be competing against 20 other '57 Chevys exactly like yours. The key to winning is in the quality of the restoration itself. So I slowly acquired the skills, and the dream began to form again.

I discovered at the shop that convertibles were much more valuable than sedans. It was at this point that I decided to restore a convertible and use the flooded sedan as a parts car. Of course, I would be limited to the same model and year. Being partial to the color red, I narrowed my search even more. However, the convertible's condition would not be all that important because the flooded sedan could be used as a donor vehicle. Besides, it just didn't make sense to put any more money into the flooded car. It was a four-door sedan and I had already spent more than the car was worth. The switch to a convertible made so much sense due to its greater value. I could almost justify to others what I was doing. Thus began a nationwide search for the elusive convertible.

My narrow focus limited my options considerably. In fact, I could only find one red convertible in this model in the entire United States. Any sane person would have let this one be, but the dream was still overpowering. I didn't care that the convertible had been involved in several hard collisions, had no floor, no drivetrain, no interior, no glass, no grille and *no title*. Looking back, I guess the only thing it had were a lot of no's. Without hesitation, I purchased it and brought it home. (You might have guessed by now that I am slightly spontaneous.) Needless to say, the jokes only got worse. However, I knew I could restore the convertible. I believe that you can do anything if you try hard enough. So I quit my job and began to work on the car full time. My father did the same, and we began restoring the car as father and son. Regardless of how the car turned out, I would still have the time my father and I spent together on the project. For a while, my fiancée (now wife) had the only income. Times were tight, but she believed in my dream. Actually I was testing to see what kind of wife she would be (just kidding, Honey!).

The convertible's body had rusted so badly that the body came off the frame in two sections. I didn't tell my father this, but at the time I had no idea how I was going to repair the body. I figured the answer would come when it was needed. So to buy some time, we went full speed into the chassis. After one year's work, we ended up with a completed chassis. I can now complete this same task in two months, but this increased level of efficiency was gained through a long learning curve. The knowledge gained during that learning curve is what I intend to share with you throughout this book.

In mythology, Dr. Frankenstein produced a single, living creature by connecting various pieces from several different donor bodies. This describes the reality of auto restoration to a tee. Most people limit themselves to the parts right in front of them. It is sometimes easier, faster and more affordable to replace a part with one from a donor vehicle. This book will explain this concept in detail. In our case, we had no choice but to replace most of the vehicle with parts taken from *several* donor cars. There were so many parts needed that we actually decided to purchase two additional cars just for parts.

The restoration techniques explained in this book can even be used on airplanes. The only difference would be in the different primers needed for aluminum. (Photo courtesy of Lone Star Aercraft)

We spent approximately one year restoring the various body parts and one additional year putting them all back together.

Fortunately, when it was finished, we had no monster. The car scored 393 out of a possible 400 points at its first showing. This was my first restoration attempt, and a high score is uncommon at a first showing. People often ask me how this was accomplished. I follow a logical, step-by-step process that dramatically simplifies the entire project. These steps can be used to restore just about anything. You could use these steps whether a car is domestic, foreign, old or new. Quite frankly, the same steps could be applied to gas pumps, pedal cars or classic soda machines. It makes little difference! The purpose of this book is to teach you how to make educated purchases; and to share restoration concepts so you can either restore an automobile yourself or know what to look for in contract help. I will also give you maintenance tips and show you how to prepare a car for shows.

Chapter 1

General Advice
and Specific Tools

The first step in restoration is research. Join every club possible that pertains to your project car. Start networking and calling club members. I have never dealt with a club member that wasn't helpful and friendly. These members can get you started, and point you to the people that have knowledge about your car. Attend as many car shows as possible. Most importantly, attend the national convention that deals with your marque. It is at these shows where you will make the contacts that will be so vital in the future. Go through the swap meet area and collect business cards of the people that deal with your year car. Also contact various lit-

Car shows are the best place to exchange information and pick up tips on restoration techniques or quality vendors.

Subscribing to collector vehicle hobby publications such as *Old Cars Weekly News & Marketplace* or *Hemmings Motor News* is a great way to research a restoration project.

erature dealers and purchase everything that has been published about your car. Dealer handbooks, sales brochures and shop manuals will come in handy later. Last but not least, subscribe to collector car hobby publications such as *Old Cars Weekly News & Marketplace* and *Hemmings Motor News.*

Throughout your restoration, be sure to take photographs before, during and after each phase of the work. This serves a dual purpose. First, it documents your work. When you are finished, friends and family will want to see the photos. I always put mine in a photo album. My "baby book" goes with me to every automotive event I attend, and you will be surprised to find out how many others do the same. It is common for long conversations and new friendships to develop from film. This camaraderie is perhaps why we restore cars. It's fun to share experiences and memories with people who have common interests. At every show, I listen to hours of stories and make dozens of new friends. You will enjoy doing the same.

Finally, photos will also come in handy when you try to put your car back together. Close-ups of the firewall and engine compartment are particularly useful. It is a good idea to

keep a journal describing what you are photographing and why. Number the entries to match the film's exposure. Make notes on the order in which parts are taken off. Make drawings of the parts and describe the bolt size and length. Record which direction the bolt faces. In other words, does the head of the bolt lie on the inside or outside of the frame? Does it have any washers and if so, what kind? Journals such as this can be valuable during the assembly phase of a restoration. When you are finished, your journal should be an assembly manual. Be sure to take your camera to car shows as well. Photograph every make and year that you are working on. I hope it is only one. Most people who start more than one project simultaneously end up failing with all of them because they quickly become overwhelmed. However, there is nothing wrong with dreaming and preparing for future projects. Go ahead and photograph the cars that appear to have superior workmanship. They can guide you as you go. Single out those cars, find the owners and ask them some questions. Where did they get the upholstery, chrome plat-

Car shows are also a great place to meet people and trade information.

When you find a restored car that you like, stop and find the owner. Get as much advice that you can. Try to find out where the owner got his restoration work done. (1961 Chevrolet Bel Air)

ing, engine work, paint and trim work done? Write it down! You will forget it as the years go by. Now imagine what you have just from this first chapter. You have the names and phone numbers of people with similar interests, the necessary contacts for parts, a complete assembly manual for your vehicle -- complete with photos -- and you have the sources for high quality work.

Most of you will want to do some or all of the work yourself. So what kind of tools and facilities will you need? A wide assortment of tools are used in the restoration process, but it is best to buy tools as you go. I've watched several people go out and buy a huge assortment of cheap tools that either break or never get used. They somehow feel more important or prepared with a wall full of tools. Purchase a tool when it becomes necessary and make sure it is of high quality. Do *not* buy the cheapest tools on the rack. Cheap tools always seem to fail when you need them most, and the wrong tools will become an obstacle to your work. Besides, your neighbors will start talking about you if they hear screaming from your garage every night.

I will be discussing all kinds of tools throughout the book, but there are a few tools that are used so often that they need to be discussed now. The most frequently used tool is an air compressor. The first thing I do when I enter my shop is turn on the air compressor. A five-horsepower compressor is fairly standard in the industry. In most shops you will also have a refrigeration unit. Its purpose is to remove the water, oil and dirt that the air compressor deposits in the air. However, a refrigeration unit is not necessary unless you plan to paint. It is important to have clean air if any priming or painting is done. There are also small, inexpensive cleaners that can be installed on the paint guns themselves. Your air compressor dealer will be able to tell you the best way to set up the air in your shop or garage. Most people put in a series of rises and drops to collect water. At each drop there is a drain to release water. I have three rises and drops after the compressor and check them for water each morning. I like to use metal pipe for my air lines, but some people use PVC. I know of only one incident where the PVC burst, but that was enough to convince me to use metal. I place female quick disconnects at various points around the shop. At each one is a place to drain water or some brand of water/oil trap.

After I turn on the compressor, I decide whether or not there is enough natural light. If it is cloudy or dark, I turn on the lights. Good lighting is important when performing tedious work. I usually run my lights so that each bank of

This compressor has a Baldor motor. Stay away from compressors that use off-brand electric motors. Also notice the water drain at the bottom and the refrigeration unit behind it.

This refrigeration unit is located immediately after the compressor. Many of these units automatically dump waste water and require little maintenance. They cost between $1,000 and $3,000 and are only a necessity if a large volume of priming or painting is to be done.

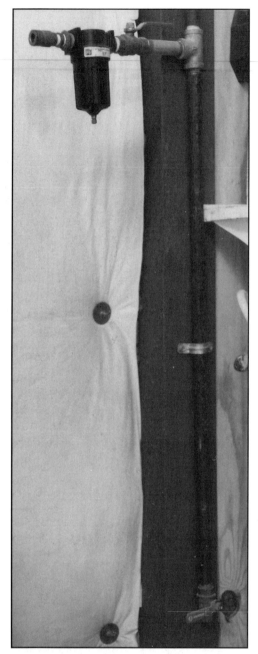

At each point where you place a female quick disconnect unit, also place a water/oil trap and a water drain down below. I hope you get the point by now that water is bad. Even the slightest amount of water can show up in a paint job. The worst thing about water is that it sometimes takes several months for it to show up. On the other hand, oil will show up immediately in the form of big craters in the paint surface. Painters call these craters "fish eyes" and they will be covered extensively in the paint and body work chapters.

lights can be turned on/off independently. This way you pay to put light only where you need it at the time.

Your basic shop is complete. Most people already own a set of tools before they become interested in auto restoration, but I will offer a few recommendations just in case. Craftsman tools have been the industry standard for decades. They have an excellent lifetime warranty. I have always thought of Craftsman as the tools dad recommends. They are sufficient for most people's needs.

However, when I started working in an auto restoration shop, every tool there was a Snap-on. I never imagined that there could actually be a difference between the brands of wrenches, but there is. Once you use a Snap-on tool, you never go back to another brand. Each point in Snap-on sockets and wrenches has been cutout so that the tool will grab the flat sides of the bolt instead of the corners. This greatly reduces the chance of rounding off the bolt. You can tell that a lot more thought and engineering have gone into their tools. I especially like their socket extensions. They have little grooves cut in the shaft to give you a little extra grip. Snap-on also has a lifetime warranty, but I have found that it is not as well enforced as Craftsman's. You have to argue with the Snap-on dealers a bit to get the warranty.

A new tool recently came on the market that's also worth mentioning. It's called the Metrinch, and it expands on the Snap-on idea. All Metrinch did is make those cutouts at each corner a little bigger. This allows the tool to fit on both SAE and the closest metric size. You no longer need two sets of tools! The idea is brilliant and I plan to purchase a set of these soon. Because the tools will fit on both SAE and metric hardware, they are less expensive than the Craftsman and Snap-on brands.

Your air compressor opens a whole new avenue of tool usage. The two pieces of equipment that I use the most are the impact wrench and air ratchet. There are many more tools that will be mentioned throughout the chapters, but I think these two items are worth purchasing now. Your whole life changes after moving up to these tools. I probably use these tools maintaining my own vehicles more than I do in restoration. It's so nice jacking up a car, using the impact wrench to remove the wheel's lugnuts, getting the job done and reinstalling the wheel and lugnuts in the time it used to take just removing the wheels. The only problem is that all of your friends will now come over to change their vehicles' oil and brake pads.

If you do not now own a floor jack, then consider purchasing one. They are not expensive. Once you grow accustomed

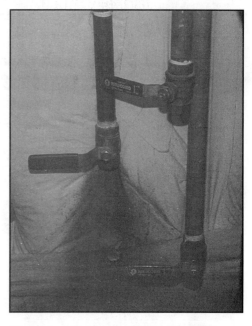

Zooming even tighter, you can see the drain handles and the water marks on the wall. These marks are black and rusty looking and would not mix well with paint. These drops do work.

What you are looking at is a series of rises and drops in the air line. At each drop in the line is a valve that can be opened to drain water. The purpose of these drops is to let the air cool so the water can condense and fall to the drains. This method is crude but a lot more affordable than refrigeration units.

Zooming in at the bottom of the drops you can see three separate drops with individual drains.

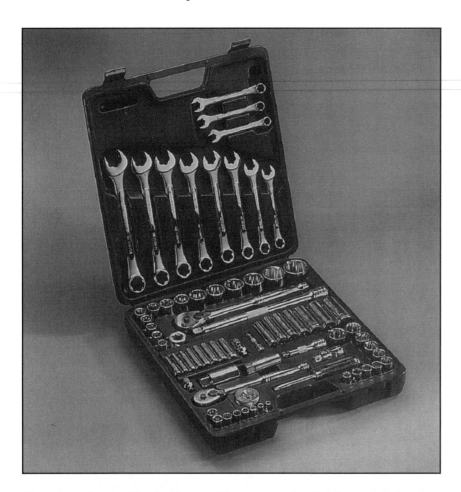

Here is a basic Metrinch set. They are affordable and fit both metric and American sizes. Their only drawback is that they have some play before they engage the bolt or nut. This means that their effectiveness is limited in tight places. (Photo courtesy of The Eastwood Company)

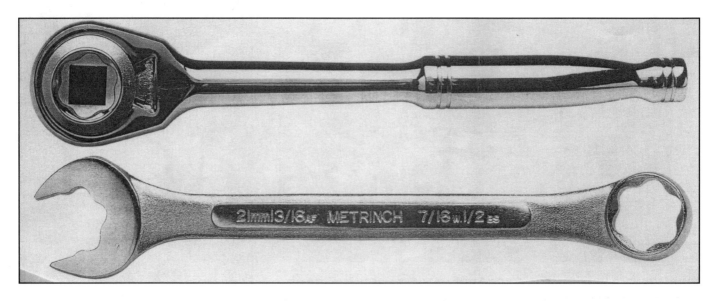

Closeup of a Metrinch. The large cutouts at the corners allow the wrench to turn many sizes as well as damaged or rounded off bolts. (Photo courtesy of The Eastwood Company)

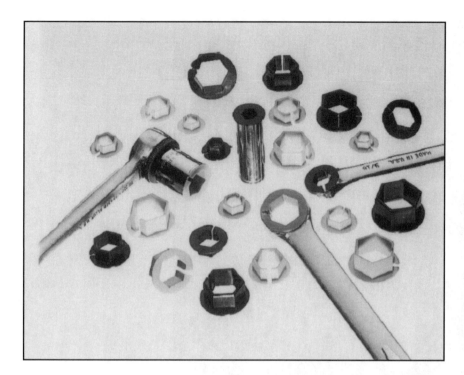

The Eastwood Company offers this set of plastic inserts for wrenches and sockets. These inserts are used in the assembly phase to protect painted hardware from scratches. (Photo courtesy of The Eastwood Company)

to using one, you will never use a scissors jack again. Floor jacks are heavier and, in turn, less mobile, but their safety and ease-of-use far outweigh their weight. (My wife is an English major and I hope she appreciates the wit of that last sentence.)

A good set of screwdrivers, an electric or battery-operated drill and a roll-around tool cabinet can be valuable as well. I do like those Snap-on screwdrivers. They seem to grip rusty screw heads better than other drivers I've tried. It seems as if I use my battery-operated drill more around my house than I do at the shop, but it comes in handy from time-to-time. I use mine as a power screwdriver with a Phillips head point, more than I do as a drill. By now, we have accumulated a few tools. By the end of this book there will be even more and it's time to consider buying a roll-around tool chest to keep these tools clean and organized.

This is a decent cabinet. I don't have any real preference when it comes to tool cabinets. All I can tell you, is that they become a necessity when your tool collection no longer fits in a single toolbox. If you have more than one toolbox or find yourself losing tools, then a tool cabinet could be the perfect birthday present. Hint! Hint!

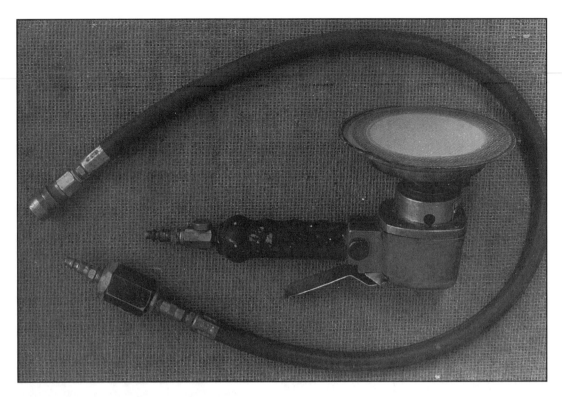

This is a dual action sander. I will be referring to this as a D/A throughout the book. Notice that it rests with a short hose with a cylinder at the end. This is called an in-line oiler. Remember that we have removed all of the water and oil from the air. Well, air tools require a generous amount of oil, so you fill the oiler with air tool oil and it automatically oils your air tool properly. This procedure gives you flexibility. You can now either paint or operate air tools from any location in the shop.

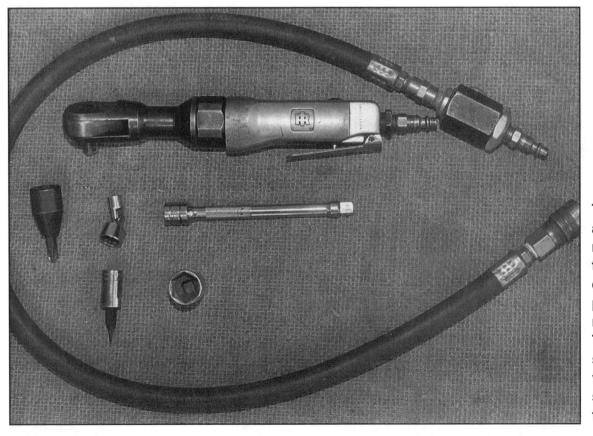

This tool is an air ratchet. Air ratchets save time in the disassembly phase of a restoration. They will drive sockets and various screwdriver tips.

Impact wrenches are similar to air ratchets but deliver more power. They are perfect for chassis disassembly, but have been known to shear stubborn nuts and bolts. You generally operate the air ratchet at a lower air pressure than you would an impact wrench. This brings up another point. Each quick disconnect point around the shop should have a valve that reduces air pressure, if so desired.

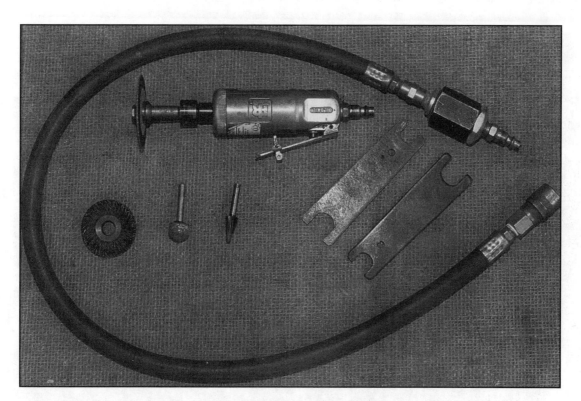

Straight die grinders are used frequently in auto restoration. The configuration shown is a cut off tool. This disc is offered by 3M and is used to cut sheet metal. It will throw sparks and a special guard is offered to contain this problem. The disc on the left is a wire wheel attachment. This wheel is good for stripping paint and rust off small objects. The other two attachments are grinders and are helpful in removing the rust pits found on exterior sheet metal.

This tool is called an air hammer. They are used to cut sheet metal. I use them to make the initial gross cuts in panels. Air hammers are not precise, but are great for releasing stress. Caution! They are loud and require hearing protection. Air drills can be useful too.

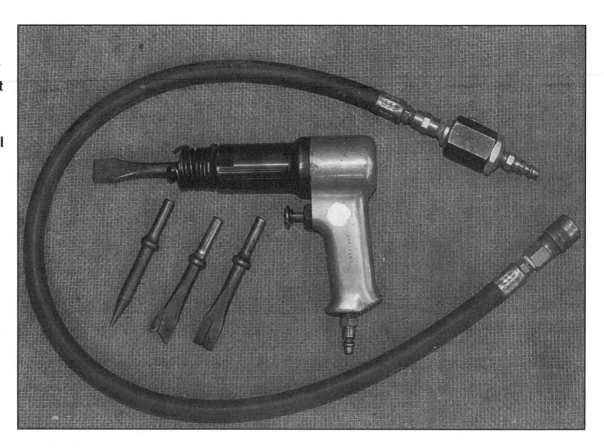

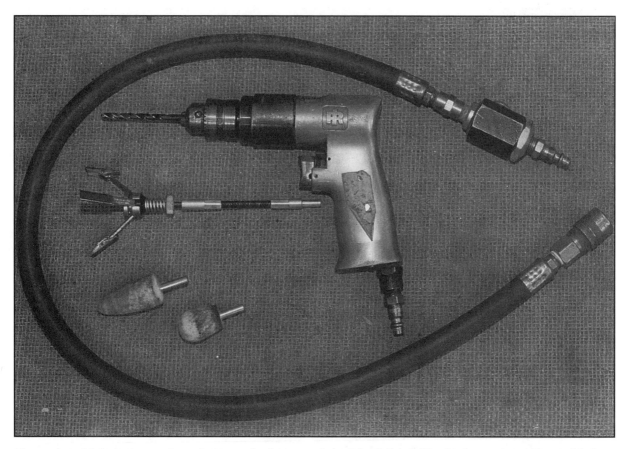

However, I have no real preference between air or electric drills. It doesn't matter which one you choose, but sooner or later you will need a drill. This drill also has a brake cylinder honing attachment as well as some small polishing buffs.

Chapter 2

Auto Purchasing Strategies

Like most people, I started out in auto restoration as a hobbyist. I intended to purchase, restore and then sell a car for profit. A buying strategy concerning an automobile's marque (Chevrolet, Dodge, Ford, etc.), model (Bel Air, Charger, Torino, etc.), color or body type (convertible, hardtop, sedan) is important in such a case. A red convertible is a desirable example of both color and body type. One could argue that it makes financial sense to spend money on restoring such a vehicle because you know you will most likely recoup your investment. Unfortunately, that is all you should expect when it is done. The day of buying and selling a car for profit is long gone. So the only cars being restored right now are red convertibles, right? Of course not. You have to factor in the human equation. People will restore a

Convertibles are generally worth more than any other body style, but they are frequently the most difficult to restore. (1953 Ford Crestline Sunliner)

There are thousands of 1957 Chevrolets, but there are more people looking for them than there are people selling them. This is what sets the price of a classic automobile, not how many were produced!

car that appeals to them or has some sentimental value as well. Once people come to the realization that their car will not sell for profit, a certain anxiety is lifted. Now all you have to worry about is what makes you happy. However, choosing what kind of car to restore can still be puzzling. Answering these questions before you begin a restoration or auto purchase can help.

What marque, model and body style do I have or want?

What is its maximum value?

How many were produced?

Is there a demand for my car?

What is the car's original color?

Does the car serve a sentimental purpose?

How much do I want to spend?

These are standard investment questions any banker or economics professor would ask. However, there is more here than meets the eye.

A car's marque, model, color and body style are important. Convertibles are the heavyweights. They bring in the most money, but they are also the most difficult to restore. Most convertibles are badly damaged from rust. Once the top deteriorates, water collects in the floorboards and often rusts out the floor completely. It will take a larger facility and budget to restore a car in this condition. In general, you will spend far more money restoring a badly deteriorated automobile than if you were to just spend more in the beginning and obtain a vehicle in better condition. If you are not partial to convertibles then consider two-door hardtops. They are usually in better condition, more affordable and can be quite valuable.

The value of a car can be found in collector car price guides, such as *Old Cars Price Guide*. These price guides base their values on the average selling prices obtained at

Who wouldn't love one of these, but be realistic with your initial investment when it comes to price and availability of parts. Most missing parts on a car such as this will have to be custom manufactured at an exorbitant price. (1929 Auburn 6-80 cabriolet)

Whatever you do, auto restoration should be fun! I had to retake this photo because nobody was smiling.

That's better! Don't run yourself into the ground. The worst thing about trying to make a business out of a hobby is that you have to maintain certain production schedules. Don't set schedules for yourself. Just work on the car for as long as you like and have fun.

both collector car dealerships as well as the many collector car auctions held around the country. They usually rank cars on a one to six condition scale. A number one car is defined as a 95-plus point show car that is not driven, and most likely has undergone a professional frame-off restoration. A number six rating describes a car that usually is incomplete and in rough condition, usually a parts donor car. Everything in between is classified in the other four conditions. True number one condition cars are extremely rare. It can sometimes be difficult to distinguish a car's condition in the two-to-three and four-to-five ranges, but it is always safer to underestimate a car's condition. Beware of the term "no rust." I have *never* seen a used car that did not have

Here is a fairly good example of a parts car. You would like to see it have an engine as well as all of the exterior trim. Try to find one that does not have a rusty floor.

some amount of rust somewhere. There should be a plate riveted to the car with the paint and trim codes on it. It is usually found on the firewall or engine compartment bracing. These codes can be translated in the parts book for the comparable marque and year. Once again, you go back to the literature sections in *Old Cars Weekly News & Marketplace, Hemmings Motor News* or your car club to obtain these manuals.

Production schedules show how many cars were produced for a given model in a given year, and current registration numbers show how many of those cars are still on the road. I hear many people shuffle these numbers around in an effort to describe supply. This information does not necessarily mean anything. Look at Chevrolets for example. Millions of Chevrolets were produced in the 1950s, but if you have priced them lately you will see that many of them are fetching more money than Cadillacs. How can this be? Well, everybody might have a '57 Chevy, but few are willing to part with them. This is what it really boils down to: A ratio of how many people are currently trying to sell a given car as compared to the number of people trying to buy at the same time.

These two cars became my life and blood for three years. There is no way that I could have completed my project without them. Needless to say, I repaid them in the end with a trip to the scrap yard, and I've been losing sleep ever since.

As for demand, do not worry about it just yet. Pick the car that looks good to you. A sentimental feeling towards a vehicle is probably the most common reason for purchase. Few people go after a car for its collector value anymore, and chances are if you like it, somebody else does too. Besides, you will need all the motivation you can get. Just make sure that it is affordable for you. I love Duesenbergs. In fact, I would have no problem restoring one for someone else, but there is just no way I could afford to restore one for myself. (My wife would probably kill me!) Also, make sure that there are plenty of parts and extra cars available that match your selected vehicle. It's a good idea to price parts before the car is purchased. This is one of those valuable lessons that I learned after the fact. Finding non-Chevy/Ford parts can be difficult. What will happen if you are close to a finished restoration with one emblem missing? More than likely, it will have to be custom manufactured at a premium price.

The car's condition is important whether you plan to sell it or not. You will spend more money and effort restoring a rust bucket than a pristine original. *This is one of the more common mistakes in classic auto selection.* The inexperienced auto restorer usually thinks that the rusted out car for $10,000 less is the better deal. This is the car that ends up for sale later because the buyer grossly underestimated how much work is required to restore an automobile. Fortunately, you will be better educated.

Sometimes there will be few or no choices. For instance, if you choose a certain model and color, you might limit yourself to only one car that is available for purchase. Of course, this means you are stuck with whatever you find! Remember that restoration labor hours, including your time, are always the most expensive part of a restoration. Therefore, the car's condition and budget go hand-in-hand.

How much can you do yourself? You might want to read this whole book before answering that question, but certain personality traits apply. Are you the type of person that mows his lawn and changes his oil, or do you always pay for someone else to do these chores? This might sound oversimplified, but this type of question can indicate a self restoration failure before it starts. Obviously, you will spend less time and considerably more money if you pay someone to restore your car for you. You do-it-yourselfers need to keep in mind that a part-time approach to auto restoration will generally take years for a full frame off restoration. A good rule of thumb to figure out how many years is at least 2,000 hours divided by the hours worked per year if no major mistakes are made. This is why so many frame off restoration attempts fail. People either underestimate the number of years involved or the number of dollars involved.

After you make your decision, stick with it and follow this advice! I strongly recommend that you buy more than one car. The second car does not have to be expensive. A good $500 four-door will do. Your research will tell you what cars have the same body, floor, chassis length, doors, trim, etc. You will need all kinds of extra parts. There is no way to tell just yet which ones you will need. I usually use two or three cars when involved in a frame off restoration.

Chapter 3

How To Make the Best Buy

It is common for the rear panel between the floor and the bumper to rust through. Most of the manufacturers loaded this area with seam sealer. We come to find out decades later that this sealant held water and actually promoted rust instead of preventing it.

Plenty of books are available that tell you what to look for in a collector car. However, there seems to be insufficient information on what to look for in a restorable or quality restored car. Most of the cars in excellent condition were snatched up in the 1980s, so you have to expect to see some fairly rough looking cars in today's market. When I go out and look for a car, I already know that I'm going to see rust. The location of the rust, however, is the main consideration. Start at the rear of the car and inspect the trunk floor. Is it even there? Knowledge of the finished product is important. What part of the trunk area will actually be exposed? Some floors are painted steel and some have a glued-down liner. Obviously the floor that has exposed steel will require a higher level of workmanship.

The most commonly found rust in the trunk area is usually the hardest to detect. I refer to this section as the rear valance panel. The rear valance panel is the central section located just forward of the rear bumper, below the trunk lid and in between the quarter panels. Be sure to inspect this area with a magnet above and below the trunk. I have never seen a car that did not have some rust in this area. If the rust has worked its way up from the trunk floor to the inner trunk walls, then I would strongly recommend purchasing a different car. It's not that this one problem is so difficult to repair, but it is a good indicator of the automobile's entire condition. The cars that I have worked on with this symptom usually require more effort than they are worth.

From there, move to the quarter panels. Have they been wrecked? You can tell by using a Spot Rot gauge. This tool is available through The Eastwood Company and measures the magnetic attraction on a metallic panel. The strength of attraction is indicative of paint and body filler thickness. If there is no magnetic attraction whatsoever, then the panel is rusted through or severely wrecked and repaired with a lot of body filler. This is another indicator of a car that is more trouble than it is worth. Be sure to inspect the bottom of the quarter panels. They typically rust through at the lower edges and require a modest amount of work to repair.

Look closely behind the bumper for this kind of damage. It takes a lot of cutting and welding to repair it and your purchase price should reflect this.

Even rust such as what's on the end of this Buick bumper should be considered at the time of purchase. You should price the car as if it had no bumper at all because it will be cheaper to replace than repair.

The floor and rocker panels should be checked next. Most cars will have some degree of rust on the floor pans, but to what degree? Sometimes the only way to find out requires getting under the car. If the car is in a field, then it's best to inspect it on a dry, sunny day. Too many people get anxious and purchase an automobile without inspecting the underside of the floor, because it was just too dirty. Remember that most of these vehicles have been parked for a long time and have become hosts for a wide variety of wildlife. However, most of this wildlife bites, scratches or stings. I fell victim to just such a flying beast while searching for parts cars one day. I don't know what protocol I violated, but a large yellow jacket came out from under a car and expressed its anger on my ankle. For the rest of the day, I could feel the venom work itself up my leg to my hip. At this point, I was in so much pain I had to go home. Just imagine what would have happened if I had stuck my face down there?

Your inspection is not finished at this point. You have merely searched for the damage caused by Mother Nature, but have you thought about the damage caused by man? This damage comes in two forms. First, there is the damage caused by parts seekers. A car that has had parts removed is more expensive to restore and your purchase price should reflect this, but it is not necessarily a roadblock. Some cars are easier to find parts for than others. It is fairly easy to find parts for American cars. However, there is at least one exception. Certain convertible parts are difficult to find. The rear seat, the top switch and the top mechanism itself are fre-

Gaping holes such as this can hide under carpet and braces. It is important to search under the car for any floor pan trouble. Some floor pans can be difficult to find depending on the model and year of the vehicle. Don't assume that floor pans are readily available just because they are the most commonly rusted panel.

What will you do if the rust hole is more than just the floor pan? More than likely, you will have to find a complete donor floor. Be sure to include this in your purchase price. Be picky and totally disregard your dream when looking for a car to restore. Your dream might force you to make a hasty decision.

quently missing. There is no real reason to buy a car missing these crucial pieces because you will probably have to buy another convertible to replace them. Few parts dealers will separate crucial pieces from a convertible. The difficulty in finding parts largely depends on the year and make of the vehicle. Obviously, Fords and Chevrolets are easier to buy parts for, but this still doesn't mean you will find them for free. You should set a limit to the number of missing parts before you consider a purchase, and your initial research should give you an idea what that number is.

Missing components is not the most serious form of man-made damage. Ironically, attempted repair and failed restoration efforts are usually what eliminates a vehicle from my list of potential projects. I never purchase cars that other people have partially restored. This is always a mistake! You also need to be aware of certain signs that give away poor repair efforts. Keep in mind that if you buy a butchered automobile, you will first have to undo the incompetent work before any other task can be accomplished. After you endure this expense, you will just then be at the point where you would have been if you had purchased a deteriorated original.

Carefully inspect the frame. Look for any cutting torch marks or added brackets. Usually the frame and firewall have to be modified before a car can be hot rodded. Repairing these modifications is usually more trouble than it's worth. Keep an eye out for pasty areas. This is a sign that someone has fiberglassed over damaged or rusty areas.

There aren't any missing pieces around this window, but wait! Look closely at this top. The vinyl top is missing near the corner. I have always found some form of rust in these situations.

Look at the bottom edges of the car. If you see any bubbling under the paint, you are probably looking at an amateur repair job. These bubbles are rust flakes held in place by the paint. By the time rust gets this bad, you are looking at a rust hole and it is not a minor thing to repair.

Double check these areas with a magnet. Brazing in metal is another incompetent repair technique. Usually people use this technique to cover areas that have completely rusted through. This method is faster and cheaper than the other methods expressed in this book, but what happens is that none of the panels are treated or sealed. In short, the metal continues to rust away, but now it oxidizes at an ever faster rate since water, salt and dirt are trapped between the two panels. You can usually spot these areas along the bottom edges of the car's body and they are rarely finished out. You will see beads of yellow brass placed around the edge of the protruding panel. These areas will still have magnetic attraction so inspect carefully. Ask yourself, "If the workmanship is poorly done here, then what about the rest of the car?" Stay far away from these cars.

I will share this true story with you just in case you are stubborn like me. I once worked at a restoration shop that received a convertible for some finishing touches. It seems that its "restoration" was started by a shop that went out of business. The car was painted and now only needed to have the trim installed. The vehicle seemed peculiar from the start because every other 1958 Chevrolet Impala that we had seen had little scoops stamped in the rear quarter panel. This car had no scoops. Then we knew we had a nightmare on our hands when none of the trim would fit. The vehicle had more than an inch of body filler on it in some places.

When the various switches and air inlet plates were removed from this car, we found the original red color. It seems that the car was chemically stripped with the air inlet plates still attached to the firewall. You will find that many people won't make the effort to remove them when a car is repainted as well.

The Impala's owner had already spent $10,000, and we had to strip it back down to bare steel and start all over. After the car was stripped, we saw numerous brazed patch panels on the side of the body. The decision was made to sandblast the entire vehicle and start over. The owner shelled out another $10,000 to disassemble and strip the entire vehicle. We then discovered brazed patch panels all over the floor. To use the term restoration for the original work would be a disservice to all honest, hardworking restorers, because the butcher responsible for this mess had done nothing more than cut out all the rusty steel and braze in patch pieces with no regard for originality. For example, there are two mounts that anchor the convertible top pistons to the floor. These were rusty, so he simply cut them out. Hello! What do you connect the top mechanism to now? I believe the body shop staff got that far and realized that they were in over their heads. The Impala's owner spent another $10,000 to get the vehicle painted but not assembled. He abandoned the project on the home stretch, with more than $40,000 down the drain. Restoration work is entirely different from collision repair. Off hand, I do not know of any modern paint and body shops that have produced a happy ending to a restoration effort.

Even more problems can be encountered trying to find out what is a car's original color. Most people hunt for the most desirable colors of red and black. They fetch the highest prices if

Remember that as you move from the 1950s to the 1960s, the firewalls change from body color to flat black. Your research will tell you which is correct.

Remember that every engine has a number that correlates to the vehicle identification number (VIN), which is usually located in the door jamb area. Make sure that the stamped number on the engine block matches the VIN number.

the vehicle should be sold. Of course dishonest sellers know this too, and frequently repaint cars in non-original colors. How do you protect yourself from fraud? The cowl tag on the firewall identifies the proper color of the car. Do not purchase a car that does not have either the cowl tag or the vehicle identification number (VIN) plate, usually located in the door jamb. If there is some doubt as to the true color of the car you are looking at, then check the bottom of the firewall, under stainless trim, inside door jams and inside trunk areas. The color should be the same. Overspray can also be detected in the wheel wells and on the underside of the floor. The Eastwood Company also sells a device that can measure the thickness of the paint. The firewall should be semi-flat black or body color as well.

Do not forget the title. This can be a headache. If you absolutely cannot obtain one, then at least get a bill of sale. There are title companies in your state that can help you if need be. The process usually requires that you put up some percentage of the value of the car as a bond. Then after a waiting period of a stated number of days, the car becomes your property. If someone else claims ownership of the car during this waiting period, then they get the bond, but you at least still get the car. Obviously, you want to start this process before you increase the value of the car through restoration!

Chapter 4

Restoration Types

What we have done in the first three chapters is plan. I know that you are eager to begin the restoration process, but planning is the key to a successful project. You now have to decide what kind of restoration you want to do. Your basic options are: factory original, trailer restored, semi-modified, modified or custom. You also have the choice of a frame-on restoration or frame-off restoration.

A factory original restoration is basically no restoration at all. To compete in this class at a car show you must not alter anything. Repainting, rechroming or new upholstery will disqualify a car from this class. You more or less buy a nice original car and clean it up as best you can. However, most competitions will allow a certain percentage of restoration. These percentages vary from show to show, but they are designed to allow for minor accident or wear-and-tear problems. For example, most competitions allow new paint on one panel to as much as one-fourth of the vehicle. They usu-

In preparation for showing a car, one of the important checklist items is cleanliness. The owner of this original 1960 Chrysler 300 is getting rid of road grime and dust picked up on the way to the showgrounds.

ally allow for one seat or one piece of chrome to be redone, too. The point here, is to review the show rules before any work is done. You can obtain a copy of the rules from the national club that pertains to your make and model. Unfortunately, I have been involved in one of the more tragic stories concerning original cars.

I met a man at a car show, who had recently purchased one of the finest original cars I have ever seen. For this particular model, there are only two fine originals known to exist. We became friends and enjoyed looking at his car. I noticed that he had done some work to the car, but did not give it much thought. The changes were minor but numerous. For example, he removed many of the engine compartment bolts and polished them. He had also rechromed many of the grille pieces. As fate would have it, the show staff selected me to be one of the point judges for the class in which this car was grouped. I had to decline due to the conflict of interest posed by our friendship (a word to the wise -- never judge a friend's car). This car, which had once been the national standard for the class, performed poorly when judged. It appears the judges docked points for every polished bolt and rechromed part. He was disappointed, and to the best of my knowledge, has never again participated in any of that club's functions. It's a sad story, but one that could have been easily avoided with a little research done beforehand.

The only other class that deals with authenticity is the trailer restored (sometimes called "restored original") class. This class usually requires that the vehicle be 100 percent authentic in appearance, but have every component of the car restored. The term *authentic* is key here. Many people confuse authenticity with originality. Technically, you cannot have a restored original. For a car to be original, it must be untouched. So what we are dealing with in this class is automobiles that have been restored to "like new" condition. It is important for cars in this class to have the original color paint, original interior design and originally equipped drivetrain. Every part, right down to the stamping on the bolts, must be authentic. New or remanufactured parts can be difficult to obtain. Therefore, this is the most challenging of all the classes for the restorer. This book will show you how to restore a car in this class. Remember, though, that this form of restoration usually takes the most time and might not be the class for you if this is your first attempt at restoration.

The semi-modified class is identical to the trailer restored class, with the exception that it allows for one alteration. This could be that you changed the original color of the car

or its interior. Every club differs on this definition. Some will allow for safety improvements such as the addition of seat belts while others will classify this change as semi-modified. This class usually has less competition and is more forgiving in its judging standards. I like this class because it allows people to be involved in the auto restoration hobby without all of the stress that the trailer restored class can cause.

The modified class is difficult to distinguish from the semi-modified or custom classes. It is usually somewhere in between. Some clubs have opted to eliminate the semi-modified class in favor of just one modified class. The modified class usually allows for one to four modifications from original. This is somewhat of a gray area so be sure to check with your national club's judging standards. Also, some hot rods fit into this class. Usually, these hot rods have performance-enhanced engines/drivetrains and suspensions but retain factory sheet metal and trim.

Custom cars usually have little or no resemblance to their assembly line origins. Typically these cars will have a chopped top, modified suspension, changes in the way the panels open or fit together and radical paint and interior schemes. Custom cars are probably the most difficult class to compete in since there are no rules. The winning car is usually selected by opinion. In addition, the winner is usually owned by the person who spent the most money. You also should know that after custom cars are one year old, they are no longer the latest thing and devaluate rapidly. I would do extensive research before building a car for this class. Read every book and magazine you can, but remember that everything you see will be out-of-date by the time the book reach-

Compared to the factory original Chrysler pictured on page 39, this 1962 Chrysler four-door hardtop has been highly modified from its original form, including the addition of aftermarket wheels, a hood scoop, hood-mounted gauges and non-factory metallic paint.

Ernie Immerso's championship winning customized 1925 Ford track roadster "Golden Star" mounted on its hi-tech display platform at a recent World of Wheels tour stop in Wisconsin. This type of display takes time and effort to erect, and adds to the cost of exhibiting a car at a show.

es print. This is what makes this class so difficult. You have to surround yourself with knowledgeable people.

I have a lot of respect for the people involved in custom work, but I shy away from the class myself. I will give you examples why. There is one pickup truck with a glass bed and virtually every metal component under the hood is gold plated. The front and rear suspension pieces and the entire exhaust system are also gold plated. Can you imagine what this cost? Needless to say, this truck wins all the time.

You must also have a display if you want to be competitive in this class. Some organizations will count the display as 25 percent of the total points a vehicle can accumulate. Most of these displays have become rather complicated. It's common to see cars on turntables surrounded by lights, intricate desert landscapes or antique garages complete with all the service equipment. Well, now you have to haul all this stuff around so a simple trailer will not do. The parking lots of these large custom shows are full of tractor-trailer rigs. So now you need an 18 wheeler! Of course, you also need a crew to help you set up and tear down each weekend. Do you see how quickly this can get seriously expensive? These people easily have more than a quarter of a million dollars invested in a car that's worth approximately $50,000.

Why is this occurring? Well, human beings are, by nature, competitive creatures. We want to be number one in everything we do, including winning at car shows. So, to earn that next trophy for the mantel, we strive to come up with some new scheme to win. This new, winning scheme gets copied by others and it then becomes the norm. The never-ending cycle continues as you must then come up with something new to wow the crowd. In general, it costs a fortune, but it doesn't take long for "the new" to again become the norm.

Not all car shows allow this type of elaborate display platform. More common to indoor events, Mother Nature has a say in what gets erected at an outdoor car show.

The result of this whole cycle becomes survival of the fittest. He who has the most money wins.

There is one final decision to make. Will you pursue a frame-on or frame-off restoration. You can usually find examples of both styles in all of the aforementioned classes. A frame-on restoration means that the car's body was not removed from the frame. These restorations take less time and money than their frame-off counterparts. Frame-on usually means that the car's doors and trunk lid were also left in place. Most people, however, opt to remove the front clip (hood and fenders) for several reasons. It's easier to paint the firewall with the front sheet metal removed. Another benefit is that it's also easier to paint the front sheet metal and firewall components when they are off the vehicle. The biggest advantage of a frame-on restoration is the time you save by leaving most of the car intact.

Time is the key difference between these two types of restoration. The frame-off restoration can take years to accomplish. It doesn't count to simply loosen the body bolts, briefly pick up the body and set it back down again. A true frame-off restoration requires that you restore the chassis and the body. You must consider that you will have to disassemble, tag, restore and reassemble more than 5,000 pieces. These projects require a substantial commitment of time, money and skill. We discussed earlier what money and competition has done to the auto restoration hobby. Therefore it should not surprise you when I tell you that frame-off restorations

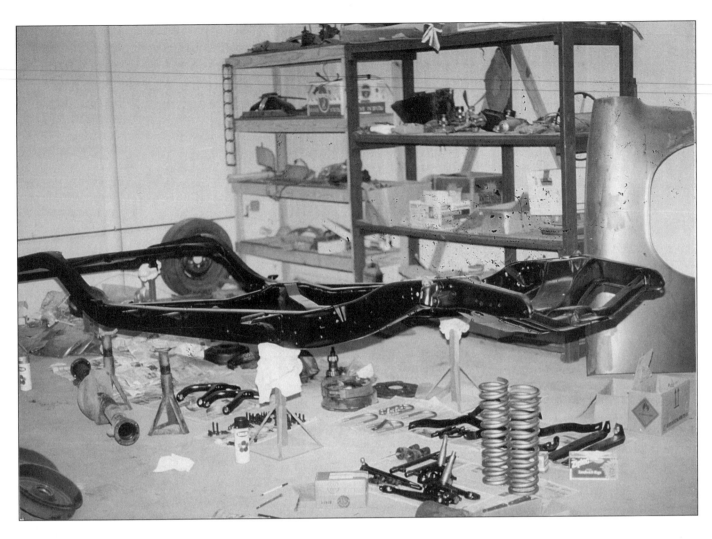

This is really what a frame-off restoration means. Every component of the car is disassembled right down to the frame. I know that some people are just sandblasting the assembled chassis and painting it black, but this is an abuse of the term. You can detect this workmanship by looking at the bushings, nuts and bolts on the chassis. Are they all black? The factory didn't do it this way.

have just about become a necessity to win in the restored and custom classes.

What is it that you are after? Is it the car or the trophies? The point I'm trying to make is that you go about a restoration differently depending on the final result you are after. This is a major point that other auto restoration books leave out. There is no one way to restore a car. You need to chart the course of your restoration project from the beginning, to arrive at your desired destination.

Chapter 5

Auto Disassembly

Disassembling a car is perhaps the most difficult and dangerous aspect of the restoration process. Taking off a fender or cutting out steel is not difficult, but doing so in such a way as to allow for correct re-assembly of the car in the future is a real art form. Most people do not realize that most failed restoration attempts can be traced to this phase of restoration. If you want to be in and out of your cars restoration quickly, then do not try to take the body apart. This process should only be considered by those who *plan* to spend more time and money, but insist on a higher level of quality. The purpose of this chapter is to educate you on the correct process so that you can either do it yourself, or know if your "restoration technician" is competent.

The body can be disassembled in two different ways. The simplest form is the removal of the fenders, hood, doors and trunk lid. You must weigh the advantages and disadvantages before you begin. The advantages in removing the body panels usually apply to show cars and high quality paint

This is a good example of a simple paint job. Notice that all of the outside objects such as lights, emblems, bumpers and mirrors are removed, but the major panels are left alone.

It is usually easier to remove the hood than trying to mask off around it. This is also a good time to replace the window gaskets if they are showing any cracks. We are using bulk plastic to mask off the windows and engine compartment. You need to place a border of paper around the painted edges because the plastic will not absorb the paint, and it will release chunks of dried paint or primer onto the painted surface.

jobs. By removing the parts and painting them separately (the way it was done in the factory) you achieve a higher quality paint job that duplicates the original factory appearance. This is important if you intend to have your car judged. Judges expect to find overspray in certain areas and not in others. For example, a car painted correctly should have overspray on the underside of the floor but not on the frame. This is because the body was painted off the frame. I also must prepare you for the price of a frame-off paint job. I would be skeptical if the price quoted was less than $8,000 and more than $20,000. A quality frame-on paint job should cost somewhere between $3,000 and $8,000. This cost does not include items in the restoration such as parts, materials and mechanical work; it does represent the labor involved in disassembling, painting and re-assembling all of the major body panels. Fortunately, labor is the one thing over which you have control.

You have to find a balance between what you do yourself and what you contract out. Everyone has a different level of potential ability. I use the term potential ability because reading this book and practicing the techniques explained within will improve your skills. Even with unlimited time, there will be a point where your skills will level off. Some people fail to recognize this and end up getting into trouble. I have a few do-it-yourselfer friends and one of them never ceases to

amaze me. He will not hesitate to get into a project, but doesn't read any "how to" books or ask for advice. He usually ends up damaging something around his house or winds up hurting himself. I think he's had more stitches than Evel Knievel. Know when to stop and hire a professional. You will spend more money repairing major mistakes than you would have if you paid someone to do it right the first time.

Disassembling a car and removing the body panels can be a hassle. This is the primary disadvantage of the process. It takes countless hours to align and refit the panels. In fact, it once took me several days to align just one hood. It can be frustrating, but I will teach you how to refit panels when we get to assembly work. Once you take everything apart, you have to keep track of the hardware and take notes on how it all goes back together. It might be several years before you start the assembly phase.

If you decide to take off some or all of the panels, watch for any metal shims that might fall out. Be sure to document their locations and save them. You will need the shims in their original locations for the panels to fit together properly. The worst thing people do here is throw away shims and rusty bolts, because most of them are not produced anymore. They can be restored with little effort, and the finished product is much more authentic when original bolts are used.

Remember what we talked about in earlier chapters? Take lots of photographs. This is the phase of restoration where you must compile your journal. Go slowly and write down how you take things apart. Draw pictures of the parts and

Many cars don't even have a frame to remove. Ford Mustangs and this Porsche are good examples. This is what people are referring to when they use the term "unibody."

A great tool to use to clean all of the greasy parts, this is a parts washer that is designed for easy service. There are companies that provide the washer fluid and pick it up and recycle it as part of their service.

Wondering how to get your interior door handles and window cranks off? Most cars require a special door handle removal tool. This tool has special teeth that grab the retainer spring and push it off. You always push from the handle side of the post to the center.

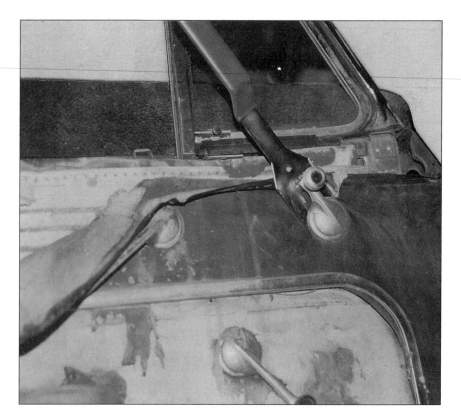

describe the hardware used. For the time being, just put the hardware pieces in plastic bags and label them. We will have to take them out later to send them to the plater, but they will be sent in major component groups. Simply put, when the entire chassis is disassembled, send out all of the hardware that pertains to the chassis. Then send the front clip, body, trim and dash hardware at different dates. This way, they are in different lots and will not become mixed in with other parts of the car. Do not add in any unrelated parts at the last minute thinking you will save a little money. The amount of hours needed to separate them later will end up costing you more. This way you will have all of the hardware parts organized by major part group and you will have a much easier time in the assembly phase of the restoration.

Look for any colored dots or slashes and record them in your journal. These are inspection marks. This transmission had a yellow slash across the top, which was added back for authenticity.

This differential was red oxide instead of black. It is common for differentials to be different from the rest of the chassis because they were manufactured in a different assembly plant.

Once again, an inspection mark was found on the rear end and later repainted. These kinds of marks are all over the chassis and will be covered in-depth in the chassis restoration chapter.

Here are three different lots of hardware. The two on top have just returned from the plater. They were separated by their location on the vehicle and sent out on different weeks.

Hot rods require a great deal of body modification. This is not the type of work a first-time restorer should attempt to do. Take the car to a professional hot rod specialist to have the body work done.

The other aspect of car body disassembly deals with cutting or modifying the actual body section itself. The most common form of this is what is referred to as a chop top. This is when the roof is cut loose and lowered a few inches. Today, you also see a lot of body panel modifications in custom work. This is difficult to do and requires a lot of creativity. Most people will lengthen the front or rear of the car by splicing in sections from other cars. This is dangerous work and I do not recommend the do-it-yourselfers to try this at home. One mistake in this process can damage your car body beyond repair. If custom work is your interest, there are countless hot rod magazines that offer tips and new ideas. There are also numerous books on performing custom work. I could go through this in detail, but I feel it would be repetitive. The purpose of this book is to cover new ground and fill in the gaps that I feel most other books leave out. You will spend thousands of dollars on this project, and there are no guarantees that it will be successful. Your best defense against poor workmanship and disaster is knowledge. Arm yourself with every relevant piece of literature possible.

There is another aspect of body modification to consider, which has become a necessity in recent years. The high demand for hardtops and convertibles has made it difficult to find viable subjects for restoration. The result of this shortage has forced people to purchase absolute piles of junk in

the hope that these derelicts will someday become their dream cars. This situation has led to most of the horror stories I hear these days. These projects usually require a partial or total floor replacement. The floor was one of the first things used in the factory to build your car. Virtually every other part is attached either directly to the floor or to a series of parts that finally end up at the floor. So a floor replacement is major work. Most of the car has to be disassembled to gain access to it. This book will cover both spot floor repair and total floor replacement, but you must first understand how your car was assembled before you begin.

Even though every car is different, there are some ground rules that apply to almost every project. You must first retrain your mind to see your car as a group of individual parts. It helps to picture the car being assembled at the factory. All steel car bodies start out as flat sheets of metal that are stamped into shapes. The shapes are spot welded together to form the car body you see later on down the road. Obviously, this is not done instantaneously. It takes a gigantic factory and numerous welding steps to get the job accomplished. Of course it helps to see the individual car, but I can

Floor pan replacement is common and is not too difficult to do. The hard part is finding the new floor pans. Any model other than a Chevy or Ford can be hard to find pans for. Most of the time, you will have to obtain them via a donor vehicle.

This is the ultimate disaster. I know you want that convertible, but wait for a decent project car to come along. Restoring this car will cost two or three times what a car in good shape would cost. I should know, this was my car and I learned this bit of advice the hard way.

say with 90 percent probability that whatever welds you can get to the easiest are the ones that were executed last.

This is extremely significant because the car body is taken apart the exact opposite from the way it was assembled at the factory. When I get to assembly work you will see that the car will be constructed in the same way and order that it was in the factory. It is easier to explain it this way:

If parts (A,C,D,R,S and X) were constructed in order (C,R,D,A,S and X), then you take apart in order (X,S,A,D,R and C) and you reconstruct in order (C,R,D,A,S and X). I hope you are not confused because we are about to conduct this exercise with about 5,000 pieces instead of six.

Chapter 6

Stripping Paint and Rust

The key to high quality paint work is the preparation. You do not have to settle for paint work that only lasts a few months to a year. There are ways to make a paint job last decades. The problem is that the preparation for such a paint job is labor intensive. This means that most paint and body shops won't fool with high quality work because it isn't profitable, and the restoration shops are expensive. Therefore, you have to do the prep work yourself or get what you pay for. I assure you the necessary prep work is not difficult, but it does take patience.

I've learned the hard way that the only way to get guaranteed results is to *completely* strip off the old paint, body filler and rust. I cannot put enough emphasis on the word completely. I learned this lesson on a small sports car I painted several years ago. I noticed that the car had been wrecked and repaired in the past. I stripped off all of the old paint work and found body filler in the front hood section. I decided not to strip 100 percent of the old filler because some of it was down in deep dents throughout the hood. The diameters were small and I figured the previous body shop could not possibly make a mistake on something so basic as body filler application. I spent the next month sanding, prepping, painting and polishing the car. Two weeks later I was about to call the owner to tell him to pick it up, when I noticed some small divots in the surface of the hood. I color sanded the areas smooth and repolished the hood. Once again, about a week later they came back. I repeated the polishing process, but this time, I polished through the clear coat. I repainted the hood and repeated the polishing process. The divots returned, and I began to think the car was cursed. I decided at this point to re-strip the hood and start all over again. I found that the old body filler was soft – it did not have enough hardener in it! I finally finished the car one month later. It only takes one of these experiences to teach you a lesson.

So how do you strip old paint, body filler and rust? There are several means at your disposal. Different methods are

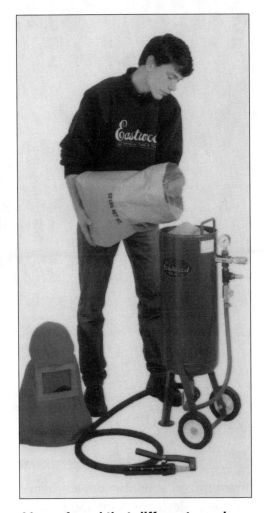

I have found that different sand suppliers grade their sand differently. I usually use a grade 4 sandblasting sand. The grains should approximately be the diameter of a mechanical pencil lead. This man is pouring the sand straight from the bag. This will work with new sand, but if you recycle your sand you will need a screen to filter particulate matter from the sand pile. (Photo courtesy of The Eastwood Company)

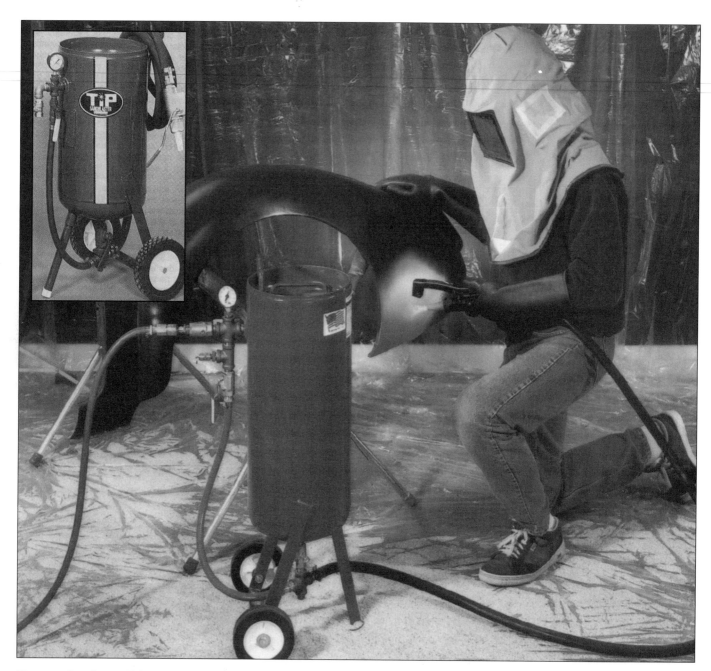

Pressurized sandblasters are used for the majority of paint and rust removal in automotive restoration. If you anticipate a slight to moderate amount of sandblasting (meaning you do not plan on doing a frame-off restoration) then you probably want to contract out the work locally. However, if you are intending to conduct a frame-off restoration then you should consider purchasing a pressurized sandblaster such as one of these from Tip (inset) or The Eastwood Company. (Photo courtesy of The Eastwood Company)

used depending on the situation. The basic options are mechanical stripping and chemical stripping.

Mechanical stripping relies on abrasion to rip away paint, filler and rust from the surface. Sandblasting is the most common form of mechanical stripping. A great deal of the car can be sandblasted. If you are intending to complete a frame-off restoration than it is probably worthwhile to purchase, rent or borrow a sandblaster and do the work yourself. Pressurized sandblasters work the best but require a larger air supply. It is also a good idea to have a concrete area to work on so the sand can be collected and reused. It is important to know what you can and cannot sandblast. Virtually every component of the chassis can be sandblasted. However, certain care must be taken to keep sand out of lu-

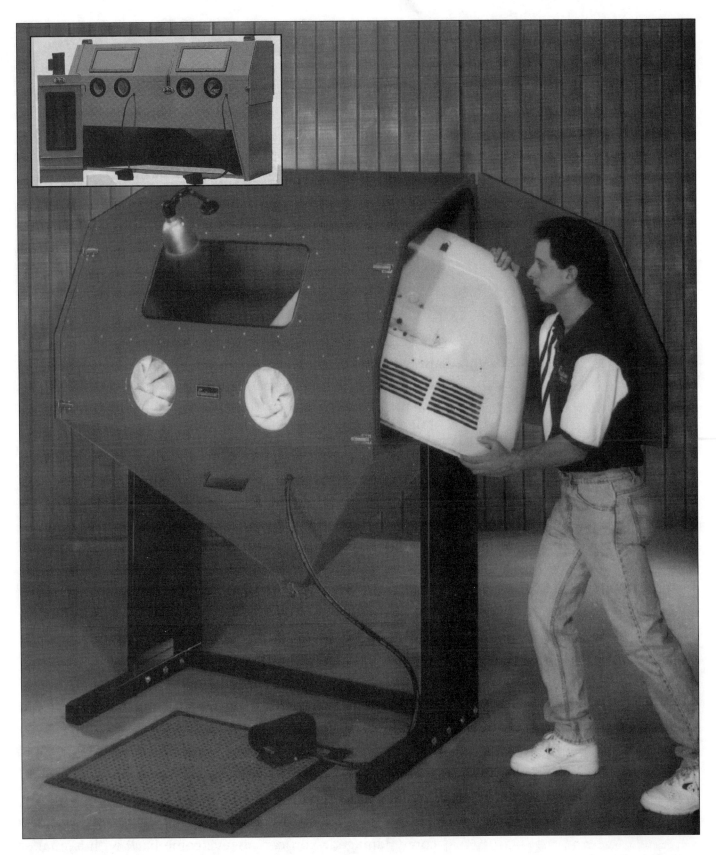

Sandblasting cabinets can be useful. They can be found in all sizes and work well for smaller parts. In fact, they are a good compromise to the pressurized sandblasters. They do not need a large open area to operate and contain their mess in the cabinet. One option would be to purchase one of these and contract out the really large jobs. Both Tip (inset) and The Eastwood Company offer a complete line of sandblasting cabinets. (Photo courtesy of The Eastwood Company)

This is an abrasive disc offered by The Eastwood Company that attaches to a six-inch grinder. (Photo courtesy of The Eastwood Company)

bricated areas such as bearing races or steering linkage pivots. Even some of the body can be sandblasted. The floor, firewall, metal dashes and door jams can all be sandblasted, but you must never sandblast exterior panels. An exterior panel is basically everything you see on the outside of the car. Door skins, fenders, quarter panels, hoods and trunk lids are all exterior panels. These panels have little support or bracing from behind and can be easily warped from sandblasting. That's right, sandblasting creates so much friction and heat that it can severely warp most exterior panels in seconds. I generally use a sandblaster to strip only the edges of these panels. I then use an electric grinder/buffer to sand the paint off the exterior skins.

An electric grinder/buffer can be a useful tool. In the metal stripping phase, I use a seven-inch 3M Hook-it pad with a 40-grit disc. The Hook-it system is basically Velcro backed items that can be applied to a universal pad. You can get numerous grades of grit in either a six- or seven-inch diameter. A seven-inch abrasive disc will work faster than the six-inch discs but there is a greater selection of discs in the six-inch line. You basically sand off the paint and old primer. This method is aggressive and can create an occasional spark so wear eye protection. I would also stay a good inch or more away from trim or glass so that they do not accidentally become damaged. You can always come back with a smaller three- or four-inch abrasive disc on a 90 degree grinder to clean up the edges.

Plastic media blasting is a newer technology in paint removal. It's one of the safest ways to remove paint from your exterior sheet metal. The downside is that you cannot do this

This is an abrasive disc that attaches to an electric drill. Chances are that you already own a drill and can use this option to avoid buying any new equipment. These discs are sometimes better than wire wheel discs because they do not throw metal fibers. (Photo courtesy of The Eastwood Company)

yourself so it will be an added cost. Also, plastic media blasting does not remove rust. This technique became popular when the American car companies were experimenting with waterborne paint and primers. The manufacturers' intentions were good, but they ended up producing paint work that peeled off within a year or so. So new cars were being sent off to be stripped and repainted. This situation has improved and I've noticed that a lot of these shops offering plastic media blasting have gone out of business. I do not use this method simply because I can strip cars myself with the other methods described above.

There are several other mechanical stripping means available if you are concerned with being environmentally friendly. Soda blasting is fairly new and gaining popularity. However, a whole new machine is needed to use it. The de-

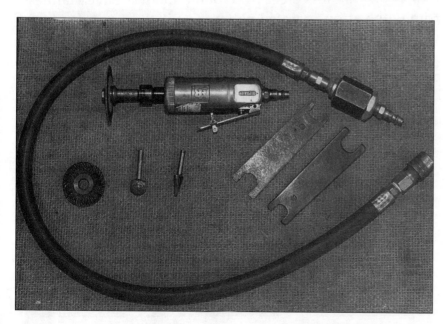

Remember this tool from Chapter One? This die grinder is great for stripping small parts such as nuts and bolts. There will be times where you will need just one bolt to finish an assembly. You can use this tool or a sandblasting cabinet to strip the bolt. Then you just paint it with paint that resembles cadmium plate. This concept is covered fully in the chassis restoration chapter.

Not enough emphasis can be placed on wearing the proper safety gear when involved in automotive restoration. The chemicals used and the airborne sandblasting particles are all harmful to you. Never take shortcuts when safety gear and tool safeguards are needed. It's also a good idea to keep an up-to-date first-aid kit and fire extinguisher nearby in your shop. (Photo courtesy of The Eastwood Company)

Oxisolv is a product offered by The Eastwood Company, which strips the rust after you have stripped the paint with paint remover. The top of the fender has been stripped with paint remover, then the middle has been stripped with Oxisolv. It is best that you then sand the surface with a dual action sander and 80-grit discs to get the surface really clean like what is seen at the bottom of the fender. (Photo courtesy of The Eastwood Company)

vice uses pressurized water and baking soda to strip paint. The water part of this process turned me off. I just do not like water next to bare steel. Crushed walnut shells have also become popular. However, you need about $100,000 worth of equipment for this method. Incidentally, it is the same equipment used in plastic media blasting and you might be able to pick it up real cheap now.

I guess what I'm confused about is how sand became environmentally unfriendly. I was under the impression that sand (or silica) is the most common element on earth. I grew up playing in it and I haven't grown a second head yet. You do need to know that not wearing the proper safety gear when sandblasting and breathing powdered sand (or silica) leads to a condition called silicosis. This is no different than fibercosis, which is caused by the unprotected breathing of powdered fiberglass. Your lungs have no way to clean or eject particles you breathe in, so both silicosis and fibercosis can cause a slow, agonizing death. Virtually every chemical used in auto restoration will do you harm, so *always* follow the safety instructions printed on their containers and *always* wear proper safety gear for the job being performed.

Chemical stripping is your other means of removing paint and rust. The most common method of chemical stripping is liquid paint remover. This is a jelly-like substance that is either brushed or sprayed on the painted surface. The chemicals in the jelly break down and lift the old paint. These chemicals are highly toxic. They should not be inhaled under any circumstance. You should also wear chemical resistant gloves to keep the paint remover off your skin. The lifted paint is then scraped off the surface with a putty knife. There are only two conditions where I will use paint stripper. The first is on stainless steel trim. Some models have stainless trim with various painted patterns on it. An example of this would be the painted border on the hubcaps of many Amer-

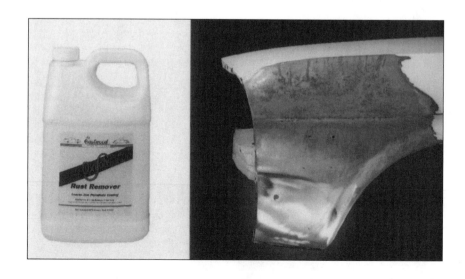

ican cars from the 1950s. Other models will have paint stripes on the side trim as well. People who try to sand the paint in these areas usually damage the polish of the trim. This is a good time to use chemical strippers. Never use them on fiberglass. The fibers will absorb the chemicals and just about make it impossible to paint the car later.

The only other time that I use chemical strippers is to clean my paint gun. Modern paints have been designed to dry quickly. In fact, they dry so quickly that it is easy to allow the paint to stay in the gun too long. Once this has happened, you have a big mess to clean up. A little paint remover here will save the day.

Another form of chemical stripping is done in a large tank. The car is set down in a chemical bath and the paint and rust is boiled off. I do not use this method either. The chemicals are trapped in the cracks and joints of the body and seep out over time. This almost always leads to a paint failure. This option is also an added cost, and then there is the problem of shipping the body to and from the facility housing the chemical bath. When it comes back, will it be primered? If not, then it will certainly rust on the way back. If it is primered, will the primer they use be compatible with your primers? There are just too many problems with this method to make it a viable option for stripping paint and rust.

The Eastwood Company offers a product similar to POR-15 that is called Corroless. Both of these products are designed to go on top of rust to seal off the metal and stop further oxidation. I only recommend that these products be used in places that sandblasters cannot reach. The inside of rocker panels is a good example. Some people will tell you that is why you use the chemical dip process, but you still have to get some kind of sealer in there no matter what process you use. (Photo courtesy of The Eastwood Company)

Chapter 7

Primers and Surfacers

This Model A has had an etching primer applied because the entire surface was covered with shallow rust pits. The acid in etching primers works well with pitted steel.

In most auto restoration books, the author will tell you specifically what kind of primer he uses or prefers. You usually see the primer cans sitting on a shelf with the brand or label facing you. Great, so you know he uses brand X number 7070. Did you ever want to know why? The other problem is that most of these chemicals become obsolete in a few years. I thought it would be more useful to list all of the basic kinds of primer available and how or why they are used. Once you understand what the various types of primer are used for, you will find that changes in technology mainly al-

Top left to right:

Activator 3689 is mixed 1:1 with self etching primer 3688 at the bottom right. This is an excellent rust inhibitor.

Vario primer surfacer 8590 is mixed 2:1 with 3030 hardener at the bottom left. This is what Spies Hecker uses as a sealer for reversible substrates such as lacquer. Primers have a blue label.

Mb 591 is a pearl base coat and is frequently used in modern pearl colors.

Middle left to right:

Spies Hecker reducers have a brown label and 3363 is used with single stage paints and most primers.

3054 reducer is used in base coats.

Notice that 8000 clear is preceded with the term MS. MS means medium solid, which refers to its solvent content. Top coats have a green label.

7799 silicone remover is the same as wax and grease remover. 7799 is alcohol based. 7010 is petroleum based and used the most frequently. 7090 is a water based wax and grease remover and is used after wet sanding.

Bottom left to right:

3030 hardener is used with most of the primers, surfacers and top coats. Hardeners have a red label.

Mb 501 is a standard base coat. Base coats have no hardener. Your true top coat protection comes from the clear coat.

3310 hardener is a special hardener used in just a few situations. What I want you to notice is that it is called HS. This means high solid. A HS product would have less VOC solvents than a MS product. Chapter 9 covers the future of paint and explains why this is so important.

Etching primer 3688 has a light brown color. Only one coat is needed. Don't try to cover the surface building multiple coats. That is not how etching primers work. (Photo courtesy of Spies Hecker Inc.)

The Eastwood Company offers a self etching primer if you do not have access to one. (Photo courtesy of The Eastwood Company)

ter the primer's chemical content or label and have little effect on your work.

You also need to know the difference between a primer and a surfacer. Primers are designed to be applied directly to the surface to be painted. Surfacers are designed to have top coats or paint applied to them. Some products are both primers and surfacers. I use Spies Hecker paint so therefore I use Spies Hecker primers. It is important not to mix chemicals from different paint companies because each company has its own chemists, and they all do things differently. I will go through the Spies Hecker product inventory and explain how the various products work. When you see a product that is referred to as a primer only, the company is telling you that it is not designed to be painted over. You must first recoat the area with a surfacer before painting.

Throughout Spies Hecker's product literature is the term "substrate." What the actual surface to be coated is made of is the substrate. Most people confuse the substrate as being what the car is made of. This is not always the case. Take a Corvette for example. The body is made of fiberglass. If you place a paint or primer on top of the old paint work, then the substrate is most likely lacquer. If you strip off the paint, then the substrate is gel coat, and if the gel coat is stripped the substrate is then fiberglass. It is important to understand this principle because the primary reason for the selection of a specific primer is the substrate. Chemicals react differently depending on the substrate to which they are applied, and a skilled painter understands these different chemicals and what substrates they work with.

An etching primer is usually necessary to get paint to stick to stainless steel, such as this Pontiac wheel cover.

It's for that reason that I'm going to go through the most commonly used primers and surfacers and tell you what they do best. As previously stated, I use the Spies Hecker paint system. You need to know that this is not the only system available, as there are several very good paint companies. I selected Spies Hecker mainly because of their excellent product support. They will take the time to train you and assist you in learning how to use their products. This applies to hobbyists as well. Spies Hecker has always treated me with the same respect as their large collision repair clients. When various brands are similar in quality and price, it's the details that eventually win me over.

The first type of primer is the acid curing, etching or wash primer. An etching primer is usually mixed 1:1 with an activator. The activator is the part of the system that does most of the work. Most etching primers have zinc chromate and phosphoric acid in them and are not safe to breathe, so only use them with an approved respirator and good ventilation. This holds true for all the chemicals used in auto restoration, so I will not repeat this warning at every mention of a chemical as long as you understand that it applies to *all* chemicals. Etching primer is used primarily as a first treatment on metal. It is absolutely required for stainless steel and aluminum. Etching primers are also good for mild steel when you have pitting damage caused by corrosion. Whenever you strip or sandblast steel, you will see that rust will return in the pits before any other area. I'm not sure why, but it does. Immediately after sandblasting, spray pitted metal with one coat

Notice the light colored areas at the door and under the rear window. These are places that have sanded through. It is sometimes more convenient to use an aerosol primer for tiny jobs such as this.

of etching primer. This prevents oxidation from humidity, before a secondary primer can be applied.

Etching primer is also used on new cars. New cars are dipped in a phosphorous solution before priming. This coating is thin, but it gives the car's nooks and crannies some rust protection down the road. Whether you realize it or not, many new cars are repainted before purchase. Car companies have been experimenting with environmentally friendly ways to paint cars. Results vary, but frequently there is an adhesion problem between the base coat and the clear coat. What the automakers have been doing, is plastic media blasting the vehicles and repainting them at the dealerships. The original phosphorous coating is not stripped by the plastic media blasting process. As it turns out, etching primers adhere well to phosphorous coatings. This is the real reason why etching primers are so frequently used. Of course, this means that many of the new vehicles are painted twice thereby adding even more chemicals to the environment than if the automakers just left the whole process alone. Did your father ever tell you "Don't fix what ain't broke!"? Well, that old lesson still applies.

Etching primers are also useful on stainless steel. There will be some stainless steel parts, such as hubcaps, that will require a coat of etching primer before paint. Spies Hecker's etching primer is 3688 transparent primer and is mixed at a 1:1 ratio with 3689 activator.

Weld through primers are designed to protect areas that will be welded in the future. Body shops will coat metal panels with this primer prior to welding so the back sides of the panels get some corrosion protection. Other primers will ignite or peel off when extreme heat is applied. Spies Hecker's

Most of this car floor has been primered with epoxy primer. This area is not painted because it is covered with carpet. Epoxy acts as a good one step sealer. Notice that this convertible has a brace between the door jam and the top mounts. This brace keeps the car body from bending when it is off the frame.

weld through primer is 3255 red brown primer. It does not require a catalyst, hardener or second agent to be added and thus is what is referred to as a one-pack product. Reducer can be added up to 40 percent.

Spies Hecker has one other one-pack product that is both a primer and a surfacer. This means that you can apply a top coat directly to its surface. It is 4080 primer surfacer and comes in an aerosol can as well as the standard gallon can form. I use this aerosol product as a quick last step right before the paint process. What usually happens is that the car will have a few bare metal spots after its final sanding. It's not cost effective to mix up a teaspoon of primer to shoot through a primer gun. You will spend more time cleaning the gun than you will priming these few bare spots. This is when a high quality aerosol primer really comes in handy.

Epoxy primers are useful in auto restoration. Most of the older cars are painted with lacquer paint. This is no big deal except for the fact that urethane enamels and lacquers react with each other. You know you have this conflict when the surface appears to shrivel and attempts to lift off the car. This reaction occurs because lacquer is what is known as a

This rear end was in such nice shape that it was decided to use epoxy and then go straight to paint.

reversible substrate. Dry lacquer can be liquefied under certain conditions. Heat, lacquer thinner and enamel reducers all break down lacquer paints. This is one of the many reasons why lacquer is an inferior paint and few people use it anymore. Epoxy primers provide an excellent barrier between lacquers and enamels. Epoxy primers are an excellent surfacer for urethane paints. Spies Hecker does not offer an epoxy primer in its automotive line but does offer some comparable products. They recommend that you use 8590 vario surfacer. This is mixed at a 2:1 ratio with the same hardener that is used in their top coats. I like that about Spies Hecker. The problem is that I like to apply wet, heavy coats. In order to use vario primer effectively, you need to apply it in several thin, dry coats. This goes against my natural priming style, and all it takes is a few wrinkle reactions to persuade you to use non-enamel products as sealers. Wrinkle reactions take a lot of time to fix so this is the one and only situation where I use a non-Spies Hecker primer.

High build or build up primers/surfacers are used during the final steps in body work. They are used to fill minor deviations on body panels and to build up a surface in preparation for block sanding. Block sanding is a process where a surface is built up with surfacer that is then sanded off with a sanding block. The low areas are identified and filled with more surfacer or polyester body filler and then block sanded again. We cover block sanding in the body work chapter so I don't want to get too technical here. You will see in later chapters that block sanding is the real secret behind show quality paint work. These types of high build products are almost always surfacers. They are designed to be one of the last steps in paint and body work and therefore can be painted on. Spies Hecker's primary high build surfacer is HS 5110 surfacer. HS stands for high solid, which means the product has a higher pigment per solvent ratio. HS products require fewer coats, contain less solvent and shrink less than a product with higher levels of solvent. HS and VHS or very high solid technology will be the primary focus of paint companies in the near future and this book covers the future of paint technology in Chapter 9.

Spies Hecker has two other useful high build products that are more like liquid polyester sprays than they are like surfacers. They are 5170 VHS surfacer and 3508 spray polyester. I use quite a bit of 3508 in auto restoration. For those of you who cannot obtain Spies Hecker products, you might want to try a similar product from The Eastwood Company called Feather Fill.

At first glance, spray polyesters seem expensive, but I assure you they are cost effective when you consider that your time is worth something too. Most hobbyists consider their time invested in a restoration project to be free. You should consider your time to cost you $25 an hour. You never directly see this cost because you do not actually write a check for it, but every hour you spend on the car is time you could be spending with your family or just relaxing. That time has a value. When I started using Spies Hecker spray polyester, I noticed that my blocking time alone was reduced 75 percent compared to when I was using high build primers. Now I strip the steel, apply the first coat of epoxy primer and then go straight to 3508. I block the 3508 until I feel that I'm close to perfectly straight. This will take some practice before you are able to identify being "close to straight" but the body work chapter will give you a few tips to get started. The spray polyester essentially eliminates several blocking steps because polyester can be applied at greater film thicknesses than standard surfacers.

Spies Hecker offers another polyester product called 5170 VHS surfacer. This product is a true surfacer, unlike 3508, and offers a high build property somewhat between the 3508 and 5110. The nice thing about this product is that you can use it when you feel that you are close to a finished, straight panel. Also, you do not need to apply a surfacer before

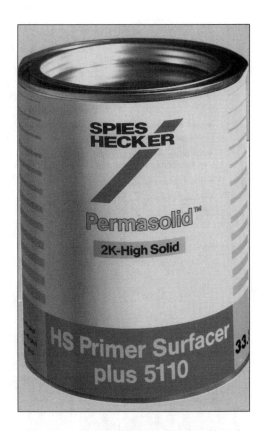

5110 is an excellent surfacer. Its high build properties cover body work and minor scratches. (Photo courtesy of Spies Hecker Inc.)

Surfacer was used on this Model A when the body work was completed. It is now wet sanded with 500 grit and painted.

painting because 5170 is a surfacer as well as a polyester filler.

Sealers are another kind of surfacer. Epoxy primer is a fairly good sealer, but it cannot be tinted. A tinting surfacer can be effective when used with a base coat/clear coat system. Most base coats are transparent, which means you will have to apply numerous coats to get the proper coverage. A tinting surfacer such as Spies Hecker 5100 surfacer can be mixed with some base coat to get it similar to the final color. Spies Hecker 5100 is opaque and usually covers in one coat. Once the car is close to the correct color, you can apply two coats of base to get the vehicle to its proper color. You can easily apply eight to ten coats of transparent base coat if you do not use a tinting surfacer. When you use so many coats you run the risk of having severe shrinkage problems later.

You can probably tell that there are many different kinds of primer. I have merely given you the spectrum of their functionality. There are hundreds of primers available that are close to the ones I've described. It is important that you have an understanding of what the various types of primer do. I have found that the products that I use change slightly from year to year. However, it causes little inconvenience because I stick with primers based on their function, not on

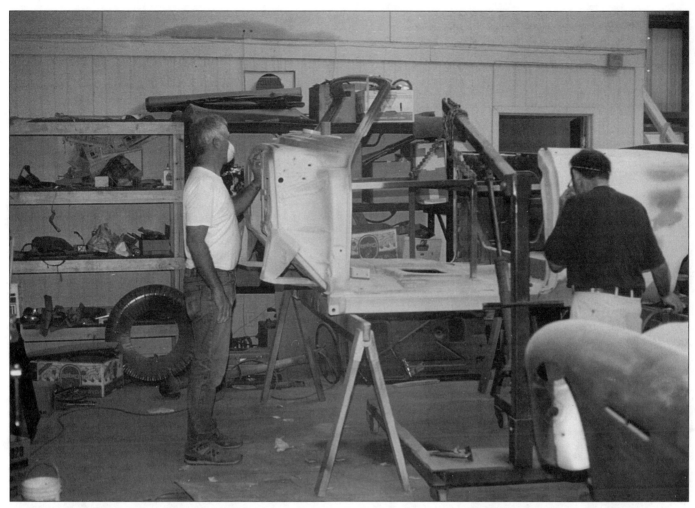

The person to the left is wet sanding the near-completed firewall with 500 grit while the person to the right is block sanding 3508. It is fairly common for a quarter panel to take a little longer than the rest of the car.

their ingredients. Let's say the government enacts another set of environmental laws that require a technical change in the structure of the primer. All I care about is that I get a high build primer, and all I have to worry about is picking a high build primer. The label tells me what the product will do before I buy it. The technical stuff is the paint company's problem. My only problem is that the price of the product goes up every time the government changes the rules.

Chapter 8

Paints

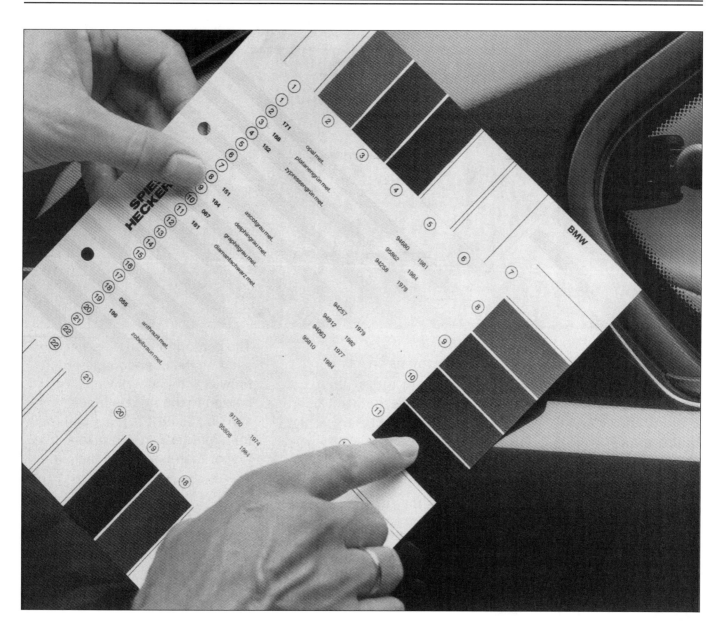

Spies Hecker has spent a lot of time taking care of the details. They have an extensive color matching system where cars are separated by marque and year. I'll show you how to use it in the paint application chapter. (Photo courtesy of Spies Hecker Inc.)

I believe that painting automobiles is the most difficult and perhaps the most misunderstood aspect of auto restoration. First of all, the finish on a properly painted car should not last just a year or two, it should last more than 20 years. I am the restoration advisor for Pontiac/Oakland Club International and I teach a class on auto restoration at the POCI annual show. I usually get some pretty strange looks after

It is common for Spies Hecker refinishers to have an elaborate paint mixing system such as the one pictured. The girl, however, might not be so common. Don't expect a paint company to make your life that easy! (Photo courtesy of Spies Hecker Inc.)

making that statement, but it's true. We have been bombarded with inaccurate information over the past few decades and I will separate fact from fiction.

First of all, you get what you pay for. I know you have heard that before, but it is especially true in the automotive paint industry. I have a friend who got a $250 paint job and was proud because he got such a good deal. Within three months it started peeling around the door handles and trim. He did not seem too upset about it, and said that he would just paint it again in a few months. Do you believe in throwing good money after bad? If one oil ring goes out in an engine, do you rebuild the whole engine or just pay someone to replace the one faulty oil ring? Much of the expense in engine rebuilding comes from the labor involved in getting the engine in and out of the car. While it's out, why not replace everything inside it with new parts so you don't have to do it again next week?

Painting cars is somewhat the same. Most of the expense in auto painting comes from the preparation. To get a high quality job, you have to remove all of the items that come into direct contact with the painted surface. This includes the grille, bumpers, every piece of trim, handles, locks, etc. In auto restoration, it usually includes the dismantling of the firewall and the removal of most of the exterior panels such as the fenders and doors. How long a car takes to prep depends on how much free time you have. It can take some people as long as five or even ten years if their free time is scarce. Most people work and cannot commit to full-time work on a vehicle. If this sounds familiar, then you are a weekend warrior like the rest of us. Trust me, spend a little more now so you don't have to dismantle all 5,000 pieces of your car again.

A high quality paint job is dependent on two things. The first is the body work or prep work that you do. There is a lot that is involved in prep work and it covers many things. How straight is your body work? How well was the rust removed or repaired? How clean were the car and its environment when it was painted? This same point applies to all of the priming stages as well. Does the paint wrap around the edges? This mainly has to do with how much of the car was disassembled before it received paint. I guarantee that a $250 paint job does not include body disassembly. What happens is that the various trim pieces are taped and every tape edge is a potential peeling point.

The next important aspect of a high quality paint job is the quality of the actual chemicals that are applied. I usually spend between $1,000 and $2,000 on the paint materials alone (this price includes all of the materials). You will need hundreds of pounds of sand for sandblasting, roll after roll of sand paper and gallons and gallons of all kinds of chemicals. When looking at paint, does the paint require a hardening catalyst? Does the paint cost $20 per gallon or $200? You get what you pay for, remember? My friend spent $250 on his car's entire paint job and I just told you that I spend $1,000 on the chemicals alone. Isn't your time or that of the painter worth something? Spend the extra money and get the highest quality paint possible. The rest of this chapter will be devoted to educating you on the various types of paint available today and what I consider to be your best buy. The following chapters will tell you how to do your prep work.

In general, there are three kinds of paint: lacquer, enamel and urethane. You almost always see the kind of paint preceded by the term "acrylic." All this means is that there is some kind of resin in the paint that makes the paint both stronger and faster drying. Each of these paints has its advantages and disadvantages.

Lacquer is one of the oldest paint technologies on the market. It has become difficult to find, primarily due to environmental reasons. Lacquer paint has a high content of volatile organic compounds (VOCs). These VOCs are what have been targeted by environmentalists as being a threat to our health, and should not be put into the air. Consequently lacquer paint is on its way out. Most of you already live in states where lacquer has been outlawed and the rest of you will find it harder to obtain because most paint manufacturers have stopped producing it. Lacquer does have some advantages. It probably has the fewest health risks of the aforementioned three types of paint. I use the term "probably" because none of the chemicals are good for you, but lacquer does not contain the highly toxic isocyanates that many enamels now have. It also dries quickly and is the least expensive of the three. Because it dries so quickly, lacquer is probably the easiest to apply. You are less likely to get a run when using lacquer than with any other paint.

However, lacquer also has drawbacks. Lacquer provides almost no protection from the sun, meaning it will likely fade when exposed to direct sunlight. This is why regular street driven cars painted with lacquer look so dull after one year and show cars look just fine after five years. This is because the show cars are stored indoors and out of the sun. Also, lacquer is hard or brittle. This sounds like an advantage, but brittle paints do not expand and contract well with outdoor temperature extremes. I once put a thermometer on

Most aerosols such as the ones The Eastwood Company offers are simple enamels. This would not be adequate for a part directly exposed to the sun, but is perfect for small parts under the hood. (Photo courtesy of The Eastwood Company)

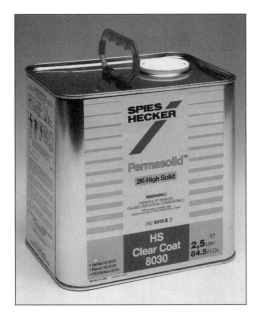

This urethane paint requires a hardener or catalyst. Urethane paints have become well known for their low maintenance, high luster finish. (Photo courtesy of Spies Hecker Inc.)

a car in the sun and it measured 140 degrees. In harsh winters, temperatures can dip to 40 below zero. The paint needs to expand and contract with the car during these times. Brittle paints have a tendency to crack under such extremes. They work just fine in air conditioned museums, but aren't of much use in the real world.

Enamel is a good paint in between lacquer and urethane. Enamel was introduced in the 1960s, and is also becoming difficult to find. This is mainly due to market forces. Most collision repair centers use urethane paints and they make up 99 percent of the market. Therefore true enamel paint is now just as hard to find as lacquer. That is the real problem with enamel. It is not as good as urethane, yet it is better than lacquer. It provides only moderate protection from the elements and it dries or cures slower than all of the other paints.

This is why urethane paint was developed. Actually it is nothing more than a super enamel. If you read the label on urethane paint you will find that it is really a urethane enamel. That's right, urethane is really an enamel paint with a super catalyst. Chemists have now perfected the enamel concept with the urethane catalysts. Urethane paint dries fairly quickly and cures with a resin film at its surface. This film is what gives urethanes their brilliant finish. It is this finish that has caught the eye of collision repair industry personnel. Body shops no longer have to buff cars to get them shiny. With urethane, they come out shiny with little effort. In addition, urethane enamels are extremely flexible. They withstand the elements and the sun extremely well. Flexible also means soft, and soft can be a double-edged sword. Soft

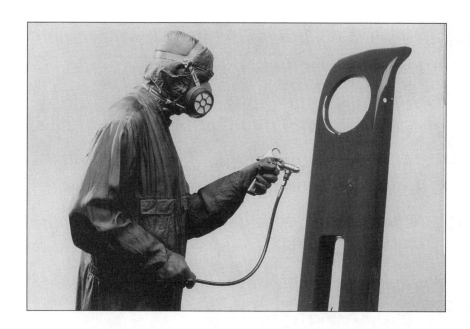

means that it is more prone to scratching than lacquer paint. Most people have learned to adapt to this drawback and upcoming chapters will offer additional helpful hints on this matter. However, health hazards are urethane's greatest drawback. Urethane contains isocyanates in its hardening catalyst. It is a form of cyanide and will make short work of your liver, if inhaled. In order to spray urethane paint safely, you need to be in a containment suit supplied with fresh air. It sounds like something the government would buy, but it is absolutely necessary. The system utilizes a small pump located outside the paint booth that pumps fresh air into a full-body plastic suit. All of this equipment is another expense in addition to the urethane paint, which is by far the most expensive paint on the market. You are probably asking, "Why bother then?" Well, it is absolutely the highest quality paint on the market so why buy something inferior? That line of reasoning can lead to certain compulsive disorders, but urethane paint is the best and I want the best for my car. Again, the quality of the paint is one of the most significant factors in achieving a long lasting paint job.

I can't tell you which one of these paints is best for you, but I chose urethane because of its durability. I have used all three and am impressed with urethane. However, do not underestimate the damage this paint can do to your health. Absolutely avoid using this paint if you are one of those guys who paints cars in your garage with a bandanna over your face!

After you have made your chemical choice, you then have to decide whether you want a single stage or base coat/clear coat system. A single stage paint is primarily found in solid colors. This would be standard red, black, white, etc. A me-

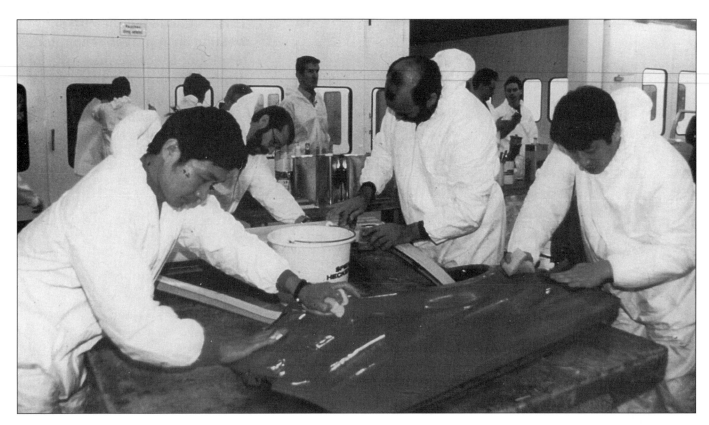

A paint handler's class such as this Spies Hecker course is a good way to get introduced to products, pick up tips and learn the safety requirements. (Photo courtesy of Spies Hecker Inc.)

tallic or pearl color would be a good example of a base coat/ clear coat color. In other words, a single stage red is red and dries to a deep gloss. A base coat/clear coat red requires a flat red base coat followed by a transparent clear coat for gloss. Why is the base coat/clear coat system necessary? Well, most metallic colors lay down better in a clear coat system than in a single stage. You have probably noticed that most modern cars are painted in a pearl system. Ford made this concept popular with an emerald green that it offered in the early 1990s. When you look at the vehicle straight on, you see emerald green. However, when you look at an edge or a glancing angle you see dark blue. Pearls are actually three stage paints. In this case, you apply an emerald green ground coat, followed by a transparent blue middle coat, followed by a clear coat.

You could write a whole book on what type of paint to use and why. Every person you ask will have a different opinion. The rule of thumb with single stage or clear coat systems is in the color itself. If your car's color is a pure color with no metallic flake or effects, it is easier to use a single stage paint. If the car is a metallic or pearl color, it is easier to use a base coat/clear coat system.

Chapter 9

The Future of Paint Technology

I mentioned before that many manufacturers produce paint that is similar in quality, but it is their product support that sets them apart. When this book was in its concept phase, I decided that I wanted a chapter devoted to the future of paint. Not knowing where to get this information, I called Spies Hecker's corporate office and asked for it. They were polite and extremely helpful. I got plenty of information. In addition, the vice-president of Spies Hecker decided to fly over and see what I was doing. I waited patiently that day in June and lo and behold, he drives up with the president of the company as well. Can you imagine two top executives of an international corporation stopping by your house, shaking your hand, asking what you think of their paint and could they be of any assistance? Now that's product support to the extreme!

This company sent me all kinds of articles about the future of paint technology. So what I'm going to do is share these articles with you. The first concept is called high solid technology. Here are two excellent articles about high solids courtesy of Spies Hecker.

What Does High Solid Actually Mean?

Aiming to reduce solvents, experts have recently concentrated on the use of water-soluble products -- primarily waterborne paints. Inevitably, this has tended to more or less distract public (and refinishers') attention away from the other solvent reducing technology, high solid paints. So, while waterborne technology enjoys an ultra-modern image, it's only recently that high solid, sometimes in conjunction with waterborne paint, has moved into the limelight.

This is paint material, as the name suggests, with a high proportion of solids and correspondingly much lower solvent content.

There are several ways of increasing the solid particle content when such systems are developed. But it's vital that this does not affect the application and optical paint film properties. And assuming it's also a question of increasing the cost-effectiveness of the system, the only way forward is by developing binding agent technology. Here, the high proportion of solid particles coupled with correspondingly low viscosity is achieved with the right choice of binding agent and thinning characteristic. This means that during the production of binding agents and hard-

You now find high solid technology in primers as well as top coats such as this clear 270. (Photo courtesy of Spies Hecker Inc.)

ening components, the development experts aim for an optimal distribution of molecular weight.

It's in this field particularly that great advances have been made in recent years. So nowadays refinishers can expect high solid application technology to match that of the established medium solid technology conventionally used for car refinishing paints. And everybody can enjoy the full benefits of reduced atmospheric pollution from organic solvents.

What's more, the high proportion of solid particles at application viscosity gives high solid technology the advantage that more material is applied in the same time. So as a rule at least one coat can be saved. And compared with medium solid, high solid reduced to spray viscosity also offers much better coverage of some 20 percent. Generally speaking, high solid technology has the economic and ecological edge over lower solid systems.

Unfortunately, there is still no standard that defines the term high solid. So far, this expression is only used loosely and like medium solid and low solid -- it has no technical definition. This means in practice that just about any manufacturer can call his product high solid -- whether it really does utilize high solid technology or not. So anything goes!

Naturally, any increase in the solid particle content from, for example 20 percent to 30 percent means a relative rise of 50 percent against the original formula, although the solvent content remains high. But it's also feasible to define the term high solid according to absolute values, or to make the "HS" description permissible only for products with a certain proportion of solid particles. Confusing matters even further, the definition can sometimes refer only to the base material, although the end product -- with hardener and thinner -- may actually be a system low in solid particles. That's why, true to a policy of fair information, Spies Hecker is committed to the following absolute solid particle proportions -- relating to the ready-to-use mixture (that is, including hardener and thinner):

Mean values, depending on colors	**System advantages over medium solid technology**
Surfacers >65% weight Pigmented top coats >60% weight Clear coats >55% weight	Fewer coats = shorter working time Improved coverage = lower material consumption Less solvent emissions = compliance with requirements Higher pigmentation = better opacity

So, as already mentioned, the reduction of solvents and solvent emissions in high solid products goes hand-in-hand with greater cost efficiency. Stated clearly: Apart from the reduced pollution levels, there are substantial material and time savings in each product segment because of the higher coverage, which saves coats. And it doesn't stop here! Right now, product versions in the so-called very high solid field are being developed in response to anticipated tougher environmental laws in California. These products astonish with still higher solid particle contents, offering further potential for savings in future.

Needless to say, acceptance of high solid technology depends directly on how easy it is to apply, on the optical results and the drying properties. Wherever the results were equal to those of conventional medium solid systems, high solid technology was readily accepted from the start. Take for instance the Permacron HS surfacer 5110 -- which, for the last few years, has enjoyed a dominant market position thanks to its application advantages plus high cost effectiveness.

However, it wasn't quite so easy for the top coats in the pigmented and clear coat area. Here the problem was the longer drying time -- medium solid products dry within 30 minutes at 60 degrees C, while high solid top coats used to take 10 minutes longer. Faced with a choice between saving material or time, refinishers usually opt for the time factor. That's why Spies Hecker stepped up its basic research efforts to develop a more reactive, low-molecular binding agent. And they succeeded! Today, Spies Hecker can supply high solid top coat systems that, just like medium solid technology, take only 30 minutes to dry at 60 degrees C. Now that the time problem has also been solved, the economic advantages of the high solid system for pigmented top coats will make their full impact. So it doesn't exactly take a fortune teller to predict that high solid technology has a brilliant future.

What will this future look like? A close examination of the two major solvent reducing technologies -- waterborne and high solid paints -- suggests interesting combinations such as waterborne paint with high solid clear coats. This is how waterborne technology can complement high solid systems. It's most likely that high solid and later very high solid technology will dominate the surfacer and clear coat fields. Granted, the solvent reduction achieved by waterborne technology in these product groups looks interesting. But they contain low levels of solid particles, which means they require more coats, plus at present they are more difficult to apply. All this makes them fall short of an optimal solution so far. – **Spies Hecker**

High Solid Technology

The term High Solid describes a technology that uses even less solvent than do Low and Medium Solid products and thus has a greater solids content. Although every paint manufacturer is talking about High Solid, there is as yet no standard that is recognized by all the suppliers. An attempt to try to define High Solid failed. But we at Spies Hecker have decided that we will only talk about HS when, for example, priming materials have a solids content of 65 percent by weight when ready for spraying, clear coats have 55 percent and pigmented top coats have 60 percent.

With surfacers the advantages of HS technology have come in useful for quite a while now: Since their introduction in 1986, Spies Hecker has continually produced new developments, which means that the current HS surfacers have become our main priming materials all around the world. The spray painter appreciates their simple application properties, excellent build and the favorable figures for material consumption.

Owing to the high demands for gloss and flow, the clear coat is a more difficult product: But since 1991, Spies Hecker has even managed to offer a technology that fulfills the strict U.S. and British volatile organic compound (VOC) legislation and that also offers advantages in its application. The current Permasolid HS Clear Coat 8030 is used in a number of body shops even though it is not a legal requirement. Along with the reduction in the amount of material used and in solvent emissions, it is possible to apply a High Solid clear coat in one go, that is, without an intermediate flash-off time, which makes it a more economical process. Many of our competitors' products go under the name of High Solid, but are not actually able to offer such substantial improvements because of their lower solids content.

The most difficult task then is to develop pigmented top coats that are genuine High Solid products. In our opinion, the Permasolid HS Automotive Top Coat Series 270 represents the high point of High Solid technology. With over 5,000 mixing formulae for solid colors, the spray painter will be able to reproduce any color that has been manufactured since 1985. The main characteristics are:

* 28 mixing colors
* all colors can also be mixed using lead-free paints
* simple mixing ratio of 2:1 without reducer
* 58% - 66% solids content, VOC value of < 420 g/1 (grams/liters)
* can be applied in one go (1.5 coats)
* prerequisite: good spray booth and equipment, spray painter must have been given proper training

Material savings of 28 percent to 36 percent, compared with conventional Medium Solid products, were confirmed in the relevant tests. The reduction in the application time by 53 percent to 75 percent was even greater. This means less time is spent in the booth and more objects can be sprayed. The short drying time of 30-40 minutes at 60 degrees C can also be reduced by the corresponding additives. With the HS mixing systems we have discovered that our competitors are calling conventional (Medium Solid) systems High Solid which of course is quite confusing.

Spies Hecker thus recommends that all modem paint shops use HS products, that is, surfacer and clear coat, in combination with the two-stage system and in particular with the Permasolid waterborne base coat system. The Permasolid HS Automotive Series 270 is designed for those who are still using one-stage systems but who still want to work with modem and efficient products.

In the long term, we would say that the waterborne base coat will be the top coat mixing system of the future and HS priming materials and clear coats will set the standards for the technology of the future. – **Spies Hecker**

The next glimpse of the future is called very high solid technology (VHS). It sounds similar to high solid, but after reading these articles by Spies Hecker you will see that VHS has a completely different chemical makeup. I believe VHS will take us into the beginning of the 21st century.

Molecular weight chart comparing Medium Solid, High Solid and Very High Solid. (Photo courtesy of Spies Hecker Inc.)

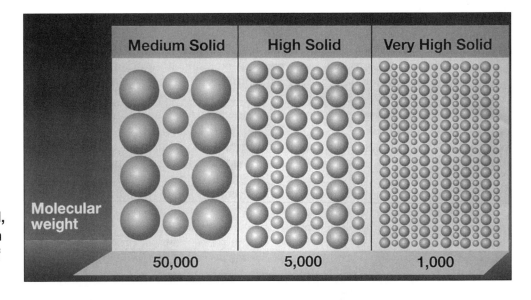

Very High Solid - A Step Towards The Future

The name itself -- Very High Solid -- tells you that these products are an advance on the successful High Solid technology vigorously promoted by Spies Hecker in recent years. Taking this for granted, it's only natural to ask why a recognized, low-solvent, environmentally friendly technology such as High Solid should already be improved, especially because it's so easy to use in practice. So why Very High Solid? And above all, why now?

First, let's look at the facts. The world's strictest environmental legislation relating to refinishing has been in force since 1995 in the United States -- more precisely, in California. Here's a law that also defines the permissible volatile organic compound (VOC) values. And it will not stop there -- a similarly tough environmental law also now applies in Great Britain and will be in place in Germany by 1999.

This induced Spies Hecker to tackle technologies today that comply with the strictest environmental regulations. The successful Permahyd System already offers a solution that makes just as much economic sense as it does ecological sense -- in view of the fact that the products on a water basis are already used every day in many body shops all over the world. But who can say today with absolute certainty what direction technology and legislation will really take? That's why Spies Hecker has developed an alternative in the form of Very High Solid (VHS) technology. It's not the water base that results in the solvent reduction here, but the high solid particle content in VHS products. An example of a VHS product is Spies Hecker's VHS surfacer 5150, available only in the American market. This product has a solid article content of 84 percent by weight at spray viscosity. Correspondingly, the VOC value is low at <2.1 lbs/gal or <250 g/l, complying with even the tough requirements of the California legislation.

Also currently available, only on the American market, the VHS clear coat 8090 achieves similarly low values with a VOC count of only 2.02 lbs/gal or 242 g/l.

However, the very high solid particle content creates some special properties: Due to the fact that the resin molecules in VHS clear coat are small, they are able to penetrate the upper surface of conventional base coat and dissolve it, which is why the base coat must be applied with the addition of five percent VHS hardener 3090. This is known not to be necessary with Medium Solid and High Solid clear coats.

Another special property resulting from the high solid particle content is the excellent coverage, and this makes the VHS products doubly cost effective. Using them saves not only material, but also time. All it takes are one to two coats of VHS surfacer to achieve a film thickness of 80-200 microns.

In short, with the Permahyd System and Very High Solid technology, Spies Hecker offers two product groups that ensure that refinishers are perfectly equipped for the future whatever happens. No matter which of the two technologies a body shop may choose -- it can be sure of using products that comply absolutely with new legislation. Which is not to say that next week, next month or in five years' time quite different solutions will not be required -- especially as the paint sector is just on the threshold of a development that will be determined more and more by market forces, legislation and research. Very High Solid technology is only one possible departure. But should the circumstances one day demand different solutions, Spies Hecker will certainly be one of the first to know about them. **– Spies Hecker**

Very High Solid Technology

1. Terminology

The term High Solid describes a technology that uses even less solvent than do Low and Medium Solid products and thus has a higher solids content. At the moment, the individual paint manufacturers use various definitions, for example Low VOC and Super High Solid, etc., when they are talking about products that have a high solids content. An attempt to establish an international definition of High Solid, which all the main suppliers would recognize, failed. When talking about products that have a high solids content, Spies Hecker has decided that it will only call a product a very high solid (VHS) product when it has a solids content of at least 80 percent by weight when ready for spraying.

2. Technology

VHS technology is a completely new technology, which is still in its infancy. The main difference between VHS technology and medium solid (MS)/high solid (HS) technology lies in the weight of the resin molecules. In comparison with MS technology, the resin molecules used in VHS technology are 50 times smaller. This means that the molecules have to cross-link 50 times more often to obtain a cross-linked and thus resistant paint film. This would normally mean that VHS products take a much longer time to dry compared with MS products. However, by using highly reactive components in the VHS molecules, the Spies Hecker research department has been able to ensure that the drying time is now at least as quick as that for conventional technology, if not quicker.

The Spies Hecker research and development team also managed to rise to another challenge. Since the resin molecule of a VHS clear coat is 50 times smaller than that of a conventional clear coat, the clear coat molecules, and this is where the process differs from MS/HS technology, penetrate part of the base coat causing it to break up, which would normally lead to adhesion problems.

To counter this, just five percent hardener is added in order to obtain exactly the same adhesion properties as are attained with an MS/HS clear coat. When used in combination with the Spies Hecker Permahyd base coat system, extremely low VOC values can be obtained thereby also helping to reduce the solvent content.

Some labels might be in German. In the Spies Hecker system, permahyd and hydro system are their way of telling you that this is a waterborne product. Basislack is base coat and perlmutt is a pearl coat. (Photo courtesy of Spies Hecker Inc.)

3. Product Characteristics

Permasolid VHS Clear Coat 8090

The Permasolid VHS Clear Coat 8090 stands out because of the extremely low VOC value of under 240 g/l (2.01 lbs/gal), which results in the solvent content being reduced by more than 80 percent compared with a conventional MS clear coat. The Permasolid VHS Clear Coat 8090 also stands out because of its very good coverage, which means that approximately 52 percent less material is required than for a conventional clear coat. With a pot life of approximately 30 minutes and a drying time of approximately 30 minutes (at 60 degrees C metal temperature) it is comparable with the conventional technologies.

Permasolid 3:1 VHS Surfacer 5150

The Permasolid 3:1 VHS Surfacer 5150 stands out because of the extremely low VOC value of under 250 g/l (2.1 lbs/gal), which results in the solvent content being reduced by more than 76 percent compared with a conventional MS surfacer. Each coat is approximately 80 microns thick, which means that with 2.5 coats, a total film thickness of up to 200 microns can be obtained. Compared with conventional products, a material saving of more than 40 percent can be achieved. With a pot life of approximately 60 minutes and a drying time of 30-50 minutes at 60 degrees C metal temperature (depending on the film thickness), all the requirements that a paint must fulfill before it can be used in practice have been met. Moreover, the Permasolid 3:1 VHS Surfacer 5150 has outstanding sanding properties. Products with this low VOC value are already a legal requirement in California and the United Kingdom.

VHS Spray Polyester 5170

The VHS Spray Polyester 5170 stands out because of the extremely low VOC value of under 250 g/l (2.1 lbs/gal). It is styrene-free and a total film thickness of 500 microns can be obtained. Products with this low VOC value are already a legal requirement in California and the United Kingdom. – **Spies Hecker**

The next concept will shock some of you. The distant future in paint lies in waterborne technology. Yes, cars in the future will be coated with paint that uses demineralized water as a reducer. As bizarre as that sounds, this technology is not quite that distant after all. In fact, waterborne base coats and clear coats exist right now! If you absolutely wanted to, you could get your car painted with this technology, and in California there exist body shops that use it on their standard production lines. Sooner or later, the government will require everybody to use it, but the nice thing about Spies Hecker is that they will have already perfected the technology when that time comes. Thanks to Spies Hecker, you know about it way in advance.

Dr. Lenhard, head of research and development at Spies Hecker.

The Technology Of The Future

An interview with Spies Hecker's Dr. Lenhard on the development of a new two-component waterborne clear coat

QUESTION: Dr. Lenhard, isocyanate as a hardener is a vital basic ingredient in any 2K clear coat. And -- as every refinisher knows -- it's a substance that reacts with water. Isn't the expression "waterborne clear coat" a contradiction in terms?

DR. LENHARD: Well, it looks like it at first sight because naturally even the Spies Hecker research team couldn't prevent the reaction of isocyanate with water. That's why we first tried to find a substance with both hardening components and the base material that don't react with water. But in the end we came back to isocyanate because the same quality and hardener properties just can't be achieved with other components. Still, we found a way of getting around this undesired reaction. We managed to ensure that the isocyanate clings onto the binding agent before it reacts with the water. In other words, it reacts with the binding agent first. This makes the isocyanate lose its affinity with water.

QUESTION: It's obvious that the clear coat is the coat that comes into direct contact with environmental influences. Couldn't a long rainfall cause some kind of unwanted reaction in the clear coat?

DR. LENHARD: No, there's no risk of that. The reason is that a new substance forms after the reaction between base material and hardener component, so -- to put it simple -- the water in the clear coat "forgets its origins." Today when we speak of waterborne clear coats we're talking about a product that fulfills all quality requirements. We put the waterborne clear coat through an extreme adhesion test, for instance. First the clear coat was applied to a sheet metal panel and then subjected to continuous water vapor at 40 degrees C for three days. Second, immediately after this constant strain, we cut squares at regular intervals in the paintwork and tried to pull off the paint in these squares using high-strength adhesive tape ...

QUESTION: Will refinishers have to change their working methods to apply the waterborne clear coat?

DR. LENHARD: No right from the beginning during development of the new clear coat we always took care that the existing techniques used by refinishers would be preserved. It started with the selection of the raw ingredients. The waterborne clear coat had to be at least as easy to apply and offer the same quality as conventional products. And there's no need for refinishers to buy new equipment to be able to apply the new Spies Hecker waterborne clear coat. The base and hardener are mixed in a ratio of 3:1 and then reduced up to 20 percent demineralized water. It's the same with the application itself: Just like waterborne base coat, the paint can be applied in two coats with a stainless steel HVLP or high-volume low-pressure gravity feed gun on either conventional or waterborne base coats. This means the process stays the same.

QUESTION: So nothing's new apart from water as the carrier material?

DR. LENHARD: Oh yes! We've adapted the base material and the hardener component to water. What will be unusual at first for refinishers is the fact that the new waterborne clear coat is opaque in its liquid state and turns clear only when it dries. Actually, this offers us a double bonus: Now refinishers can see straight away whether they've applied paint all over, plus they know whether the clear coat is already dry or not.

QUESTION: But what about the flash-off and drying times of the paint?

DR. LENHARD: Well, right now we can't give any final answers on this, because the product is still in the development stage. Available now is the first generation, and the emphasis here was primarily on its use -- we wanted the application to be comparable to that for conventional paints. More development work will be required before we can really make comparisons of all aspects.

QUESTION: And what will the final result be like?

DR.LENHARD: Even today the result is so good that we can already use it, but we'll continue to work on it.

QUESTION: Does this mean there will be a change-over to waterborne clear coat?

DR. LENHARD: No -- or at least, a direct change-over is not currently planned at Spies Hecker. But customers who are interested can try out the waterborne clear coat at Spies Hecker right now. That way, both sides can learn something and we can test the real market potential of the product. After all, it's part of the company philosophy at Spies Hecker that we cooperate with our customers as partners to find optimum solutions.

QUESTION: So the changeover is only a question of time?

DR. LENHARD: That depends on a lot of factors. One of them, as I already mentioned, is the technical maturity, but another is the legislators. Should the use of waterborne clear coat one day be statutorily prescribed, then Spies Hecker will be able to offer body shops an advanced product that can be applied easily and efficiently. Incidentally, this is the main reason why Spies Hecker has developed a waterborne clear coat now. The way we at Spies Hecker see it: Working together in partnership also means that we recognize developments in legislation and technology and act on them in good time.

QUESTION: And what's the advantage for refinishers who try out waterborne clear coat at this early stage?

DR. LENHARD: You see, although we developed the waterborne clear coat closely in keeping properties similar to conventional paints. It is and remains a new product and in practice it takes a while to become used to it. So it's definitely a good idea for our customers to gain experience with waterborne clear coat at leisure and to communicate with Spies Hecker. One day, when waterborne clear coat is required by law, they'll already have sufficient knowledge about the properties and the application of the product to accomplish the change-over without any problems. This smooth transition is important because car owners above all expect good paintwork results and on-the-dot delivery -- so there's no room for delays. That's why it will pay to become acquainted with waterborne clear coat at an early, date -- even without any legal necessity. **– Spies Hecker**

Waterborne Paint Technology

Along with many other developments, waterborne paint technology is a future-orientated development.

Waterborne products for refinishing have the big advantage that they meet the current specifications for new developments that are becoming increasingly important:

* Conservation by drastic reductions in organic solvents
* Safety by using water instead of easily flammable reducers
* Active participation in the race for new technologies in the automobile sector

With the successful development of such waterborne paint systems, Spies Hecker throws open wide the window to the future.

As an innovative supplier, when it comes to developing paint Spies Hecker holds two principles to be true:

1. We provide the specialist companies with new products that have been perfected and that are now ready for the market, for example, waterborne base coat.
2. When it comes to new systems, we work in close cooperation with our customers, the specialist companies, even in the early development stages, for example, waterborne clear coat.

So what does this mean on a practical level:

With the waterborne base coat, we have already successfully employed both of these principles.

The signals we received from our customers were:

The application and drying times must be kept as short as possible, for reasons of costs.

The color mixing processes must be kept as simple as possible in order to achieve the best results as regards quality assurance.

The color range must be complete so that any repair can be carried out using just one system. After all, it would be uneconomical to have two base coat systems running in parallel.

With the Permahyd base coat, Spies Hecker met all three requirements.

The system is one of the "quickest" and, as far as the mixing components are concerned, one of the most efficient. With 15,000 colors it meets all the current needs.

With the waterborne clear coat we are well on the way to developing an innovative product.

Despite the restrictive "reality of the market situation," we have already met the most impossible demands: Permahyd 2K clear coat can be prepared and applied in the same way as the conventional Permacron clear coats.

As a result of the current cooperation with Spies Hecker's innovative customers, Spies Hecker will provide the painter with a product that, in the medium term, will be ready for the market. With this we are opening up the future for vehicle refinishing in a complete waterborne paint system. – **Spies Hecker**

The Specific Properties Of Waterborne Paint

It's well known that waterborne paint has a reduced solvent content. But how does it work? And what makes waterborne paints different from conventional paint resins?

The Difference Between Conventional Paint Resins And Waterborne Paint Systems

The obvious difference is the most visible one: Conventional paint resins are soluble in organic solvents. The solution thus achieved is clear and does not diffuse light (the so-called Tyndall effect). Contrastingly, waterborne resin systems (emulsions) are soluble in water, have a cloudy to milky appearance and a strong Tyndall effect.

Yet that's not the only difference. A paint film produced from a resin solution and physically dried can subsequently be dissolved in organic solvents. Unlike paint films from a resin emulsion -- these are not water-soluble.

The Secret Of Waterborne Paints: The Emulsifier

There's a simple experiment that demonstrates why resin emulsions are not water-soluble. Anybody who has attempted to mix water and petrol knows that, once you stop shaking it, the heavier water sinks to the bottom and the lighter petrol "floats" on the surface of the water. The two liquids have separated.

Add an emulsifier, and the result is startlingly different. Then the two liquids combine to form a stable mixture called an emulsion.

So an emulsifier is a substance that allows us to create a stable mixture from two incompatible liquids. That's the basic prerequisite for a waterborne paint.

How Does The Coat Of Paint Form?

When the base coat dries and the water evaporates, the resin droplets move closer together. This initially forms a dense layer of tiny balls with water remaining only in the spaces in between. Finally, when the water has evaporated completely, the resin droplets blend into a closed, irreversible (that is, not water-soluble) film. What is important for the properties of this film is the degree of blending together. To assist this process, small amounts of organic solvents, among other things, are added. They are called co-solvents. That's why most waterborne paints still contain up to 10 percent solvents. All the same, waterborne paint does represent a giant step in solvent reduction, considering that a conventional base coat contains between 85 percent and 88 percent solvents.

How Well And How Quickly Do Waterborne Paints Dry?

That depends largely on the relative humidity. The warmer the air is, the more moisture it generally contains. Refinishers can influence the drying process by regulating various factors: the temperature, the relative air humidity (which can be controlled by the temperature) and the air speed.

Naturally, if the relative humidity is too high, the flash-off time will increase. Conversely, where the relative humidity is too low there is a danger that the absorption of overspray is impaired, because then the paint overspray dries before it hits the object and can no longer blend there.

Even with a high relative humidity (under 100 percent), a strong movement of air on the object's surface assists the drying process.

What External Conditions Must Be Observed When Working With Waterborne Paints?

Particularly important for working with an emulsion (that includes waterborne paints) is the temperature. Seen from a purely physical angle, the temperature of a substance is nothing more than the oscillation energy of the molecules -- the higher the temperature, the stronger the oscillations. Whenever the surrounding temperature is just right, this phenomenon contributes to the stabilization of the emulsion, but frost or extremely high temperatures cause problems. They alter the structure of the paint and cause inferior quality. This is why waterborne paints must be stored at the specified temperatures -- not under +5 degrees C and not over +30 degrees C.

Adding acids or minerals (such as you find in tap water, for instance) to an emulsion destroys the effect of the emulsifier. The emulsion breaks down and flocculation occurs. So it's essential to dilute waterborne paints with fully demineralized water -- so-called VE water -- and on no account with tap water. – **Spies Hecker**

Well, that's a look at the future. I wouldn't be fearful of change. This waterborne movement is going to happen. I imagine that many people complained when automakers first switched from lacquer to enamel paint. The only concern is when government mandates technology before its time.

This pile isn't so overwhelming now. (Photo courtesy of Spies Hecker Inc.)

Chapter 10

Removing the Body and Restoring the Chassis

Body removal is not difficult, but a strategy and forethought are needed to do it successfully. Body-off (usually called frame-off) restorations will certainly triple the amount of work involved for the entire project, so think about this before you start tearing into things. Frame-off restorations are only necessary when the owner is determined to enter his car in competition. I have received countless letters and phone calls from people who want frame-off restorations, but have no intention of showing their cars. In almost every case, you will spend more on a frame-off restoration than the car will be worth. So why do people do it? A frame-on restoration simply cannot compete with a frame-off at a show. Therefore, this chapter is only relevant for those of you who intend to show your car more than you intend to drive it.

Your first step is to remove the doors, but a couple of tools are necessary to complete the task. Depending on the year of the car, there is a special tool used to remove the door and window crank handles. This tool allows you to remove the spring tension clips that hold the handles in place. The clips can be found between the handle and the large spacing washer behind the handle. Once the door handles have been removed, the next step is to figure out how the door panels are attached. Cars from the 1950s usually have metal nails that stick into slots on the door's edge. Door panels from the 1960s and 1970s have a metal clip that snaps into a hole on the door. In both cases, there is a special tool (which looks

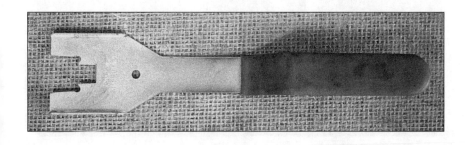

This is a Snap-On door handle remover. Once the clip has been pushed off, the handle pulls straight off of the door.

The clips are usually pushed off in this direction.

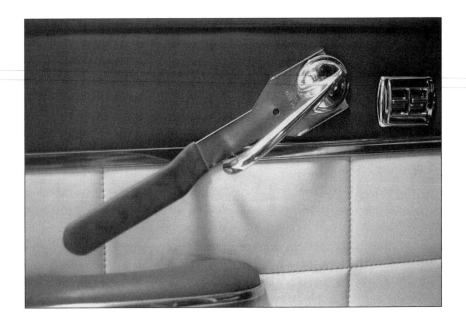

like a glorified screwdriver) that can be used to pry the panel away from the door. Sometimes there are sheet metal screws here and there, so the rule of thumb is to go slowly. For instance, only attempt to pry the panel halfway off all around, then inspect for screws and continue. With most makes, you will first remove the door from the hinge. I recommend that you have an assistant hold the door while you loosen the bolts. It is a good idea to remove the door with everything still in place inside. You will restore the doors later and it's better to leave them intact. This way you will not forget how

Shims usually can be found at the fender mounting holes.

Don't get lazy and cut these wires. Usually there are special light sockets and clips that can be found on the original wiring harness. In most cases, new harnesses will be missing these special attachments. If these are cut away, you also will have no reference to reinstall the harness.

to put things back together or lose critical parts among the huge pile you are about to create. I also recommend that you leave the hinge attached to the car. It is difficult to align a door hinge, and if you leave it alone you at least have the factory alignment. This is a good time to replace the door hinge pins and bushings as well.

With an assistant, next remove the trunk lid. There are usually no more than four bolts holding it on. Be sure to note in your journal whether or not these bolts are painted. They almost always are. This is because most factories painted cars with their trunk lids and doors already installed. Most restorers fail to duplicate this and their cars lose points as a result.

The hood can now be removed. This is a fairly awkward job and I like to have three people to remove a hood. An air ratchet really comes in handy during the disassembly phase. Your two assistants will be supporting the weight of the hood and will be waiting on you to remove the last bolt. The longer it takes you to remove the bolts, the more likely someone will make a mistake. The first hood I removed, I didn't have any help and attempted the procedure alone. I ended up putting a dent on one fender and two dents in the hood. They are heavier than they look.

Next the fenders, inner fender wells and grille need to be removed. This is where the advice in Chapter 5 becomes re-

Imagine trying to sandblast the inside of this body when it is four feet in the air.

Here is a simple body dolly. Notice that the body is on six-inch risers. These risers are bent 90 degrees on top to distribute the body's weight over a greater area.

ally important. Notes need to be made in your journal throughout this entire process. After the front clip has been removed, it will then be clear which wires, cables, etc., need to be removed for the firewall to have a clean break from the frame. Now get under the car and remove all of the body mount bolts. Of course, unibody cars do not have a frame to separate. A Ford Mustang is a good example of such a car. People with unibody cars need only to restore the underside of the floor and the suspension of their show cars.

You next need to decide what you are going to do with the body once you have separated it from the frame. You have three basic options. First, you can restore the body on sawhorses. Once the body is off the frame, it is set and restored on sawhorses. This is the most affordable, but also most dangerous and difficult way to restore a car body. It is unstable, immobile and difficult to access while perched several feet off the ground. Another way to approach this is with a car dolly. You basically manufacture a box frame that is a foot shorter in width and length than the dimensions of the body. Attach casters at each corner, as well as a six-inch riser at each corner and you have a dolly. This is one of the most economical and safe ways to restore a car body. The best and most expensive way is to build or purchase a body rotisserie. This is a large frame mechanism that holds a car body in the air in such a way as to allow it to be rotated 360 degrees in midair. The rotisserie is also set on four casters so that the body can be pushed around. When sandblasting or painting a car, the rotisserie is what most professional restorers use, but they are not mandatory. They cost several thousand dol-

A rotisserie is wonderful when you do this kind of work on a daily basis. Imagine trying to weld on this floor with the sparks showering down on you.

lars and I do not recommend them for the hobbyist or the one-time restorer. I would only recommend a rotisserie to those of you who intend to restore more than one car.

Prior to removing the body from the car, measure the car's width from the outside of the tires and make two sawhorses that are at least six inches wider than the width of the car. The overall height of the horses needs to be just slightly higher than the tires. The idea here is that once the body is lifted, it rests on the sawhorses in such a fashion as to allow the chassis to be rolled out smoothly.

Now comes the tricky part – lifting the body. There are numerous ways to accomplish this, but without seeing your car I will give you some ideas and let your creativity handle the rest. Generally, the body is tilted from front to back with an engine hoist. This is done by lifting the front first and setting it on a sawhorse, then repeating the process for the rear of the car. If you have a convertible, be sure to build a brace that bolts from the leading door jam to the top mounting braces. It is important that the brace be extremely strong and it must fit tightly in place. This brace keeps the car body from folding in half when lifted. Those of you with convertibles should not underestimate the importance of this step. I've seen several people damage their cars beyond repair during the body removal process. Just because the body doesn't appear to fold does not mean that it hasn't bent just enough to make door installation impossible. If you are having trouble finding a reinforced area on the firewall that the hoist can be fastened to, then a brace can usually be made that bolts to the firewall in some fashion. The top of this brace is then fitted with a hook or loop for the hoist. In the trunk area, you can usually run bolts with large washers through the gas tank

This lifting method works well. Notice that the sawhorses are just wider than the tires and that the engine hoist is attached to a brace at the center of the body.

Some bodies are light enough in the back for three people to just lift the rear without the aid of a hoist. A fourth person is needed to place the sawhorse.

mounting holes, attach chains to the bolts and connect the chains to the hoist. I like to use some rubber between the washers and the car to prevent damage.

Other methods of body removal incorporate ancient lifting techniques. If you can muscle the body high enough to get some long two-by-fours under width-wise, you and your buddies could lift the body in a fashion similar to ancient servants carrying their king's throne. One other method, building a sling, could also be used. This can be done by running tow straps under the body to build a kind of cradle. The

A convertible brace is being manufactured here. The brace is attached to the convertible top mounting braces behind the rear seat, down to the front seat braces on the floor and will next be bolted to the front door hinges.

Another view of a convertible inner brace. The front portion of the brace is not welded but bolted to the center bar. This allows for easier removal after the body has been painted.

hoist then can be attached to the straps to achieve lift. Whatever you do, be sure that the straps do not touch the sides of the car (the sling should resemble a square instead of a triangle). Otherwise the straps will crush the sides of the body. Remember that the rocker panels act as the spinal column for

Convertible bodies are actually easier to remove than sedan bodies because the center brace is a perfect lifting point.

This is not magic. The body is hanging from a hoist on the ceiling. I have found this to be the easiest method of all. Notice that just one person can accomplish the task. The entire area beneath is free. A rotisserie can now be moved in from the side. Other methods require that the rotisserie be disassembled and brought in from the ends.

The body can now be lowered on a dolly for body work.

The body can be placed in a rotisserie for underneath work. This floor can now be easily sandblasted.

This body is using an extra chassis as a dolly. This is perhaps the cheapest and easiest method of all.

The chassis is rolled clear and the body has been put in a rotisserie (background).

the entire body; if they are fairly rusty, you should take a look at the rust repair chapter and mend them before any lifting is done.

The method I use now requires a reinforced roof or metal building. I have a chain hoist mounted on a rafter of my metal building. Most of the cars I restore are convertibles and I attach the hoist's chain to the center of the convertible bracing. Then I just lift the body into the air and push out the chassis. Once the chassis is pushed out of the way, you can store the body on sawhorses, a dolly or in a rotisserie until the chassis has been restored.

Obviously you have to think about this for a while, and there are many other ways to approach it. Whatever you do, do not get under the car at any point of the lifting process. The car body is heavier than it looks.

Once the chassis is free, I like to concentrate on the chassis until it is finished. There are two reasons for this. The first is logistics. Try to disassemble as little of the car as possible and finish restoring each component before you move on to the next. This strategy helps prevent the loss of parts and helps keep the parts' locations fresh in your mind.

Disassemble the chassis slowly. Be sure to record where everything goes and the direction the bolts are facing. I keep a recorded description of the bolts and their location so the chassis can be reassembled as easily as possible. It's a good idea to lay out the parts around the chassis and photograph them. This can prove to be a useful addition to your journal.

Unfortunately, this chassis has been spray painted sometime in its life. This happens often and prevents recovery of almost all accurate information concerning authenticity. You have no choice but to look for information in wrecking yards as well as on other restored cars.

Look for any remaining cadmium or black oxide plating on the hardware pieces as well. Then sort the hardware into two separate lots so they can be sent out for replating. I replate all of the cadmium parts with new clear cadmium plate, but I prefer black zinc plate to black oxide. This is not 100 percent original in appearance, but black zinc is much more durable. I have found that black oxide bolts can show oxidation within a year and the black zinc fades to a black oxide appearance within a few months anyway.

When dealing with rusty hardware pieces, it is a good idea to sandblast them beforehand. This will help ensure proper plating adhesion. A blasting cabinet is generally the tool of choice in this situation because the parts are too small for a pressurized sandblaster. However, I eventually decided to pay the plater to also strip the bolts because it became too time consuming. It can take a whole day to blast one batch of hardware parts. The extra cost is minimal and your time can be better used elsewhere.

Look for any colored paint marks on the suspension parts. These are factory inspection marks. When the car was finished, it was inspected for safety. This generally meant that the bolts were checked to see if they were properly tightened. The people in charge of the inspection would leave different colored marks as proof that the work had been done.

If you find any, be sure to record their location and color because this process will be duplicated for authenticity.

Most fuel and brake lines can be purchased new. However with many of the more rare or unusual marques, you will have to send your old lines to a line manufacturer. There are at least two companies that advertise in *Old Cars Weekly News & Marketplace* and *Hemmings Motor News* that offer this service. Call them to check availability and get advice on how to ship your lines for duplication. You have a choice between mild or stainless steel. Stainless is a little more expensive but it will keep its "like new" appearance where mild steel will rust, just like the original line you are replacing. I would also recommend sending your brake cylinders to White Post Restorations in White Post, Virginia, to have them honed and sleeved in brass.

Every part on the chassis is sandblasted with a pressurized sandblaster. Certain care must be taken with a few of the parts. The rearend and differential should be blasted when they are still bolted together (assuming the differential is not aluminum). Sand is going to get all over the place, so think beforehand. Certain parts in the steering linkage (such as tie rod ends) move and rotate in a socket. To prevent sand from getting down in the socket, I tape the exposed socket area with strong plastic or Teflon tape (try the hardware store). You also do not want to sandblast bearings, races or the insides of wheel drums.

You now must decide whether or not you want to paint or powder coat your chassis components. The discussion of which is the best and why has almost taken the place of whether a Ford is better than a Chevy. Everybody seems to have an opinion on this matter.

Powder coating is by far much harder and more scratch resistant than paint. It is also more friendly to the environment in the sense that it contains no solvents or reducers. It is also almost "idiot proof" to apply. There is no question as to whether enough product has been applied nor any problem with runs. It costs about the same to have done as painting, but the problem is that there is no way you can do it yourself. No matter what, powder coating will be an added cost and make the restoration more expensive. You do not have to pay someone to paint your chassis parts, because you can do it yourself. Another problem with powder coating is that it requires a lot of heat to apply. This means that the areas that it can be applied to are rather limited. You also cannot put any body filler or primer underneath it. If you happen to have rust pits or any grooves in the steel, you can fill them with body filler, sand smooth and paint to obtain a "like

Disassembling the front suspension is dangerous work, but a few simple procedures are known to make the task both easier and safer.

The most dangerous part concerns the front coil springs. They are under tremendous tension and will launch out of their spring pockets when disassembled incorrectly. I know of one person who broke his collarbone doing this task incorrectly. The best method I have found utilizes a chain and a floor jack. The chain is wrapped around the top of the control arm and under the jack. The chain is bolted together and the jack is pumped up to slightly compress the coil spring.

Make sure the chain is under the floor jack's frame. Once the jack starts to compress the spring, the lower control arm can be unbolted from the frame. Then, slowly let down the jack, and pull out the spring. It's that easy! The upper control arm can now be unbolted and the suspension removed as one piece.

new" appearance. There is no practical way to accomplish this with powder coating. This is why most powder coated frames appear pitted and rough. Because of this one drawback, I currently prefer paint over powder coating.

Once the entire chassis is disassembled, you begin with the frame. Logistically, it is much easier to restore the central most part and then restore the parts that attach to it. This way you are not storing finished parts and waiting for them to become scratched. Once the secondary parts have been restored, you just bolt them in place.

The rear leaf springs unbolt at the front and rear with either a single bolt or a shackle. The whole unit can be dropped down with a floor jack. You'll soon realize that it is extremely heavy, so don't use your back. I recommend that you restore the frame and then restore the individual components. It is easier to keep track of the parts that way.

Most frames will have some kind of man-made damage. This frame had a trailer hitch and a bent rear frame rail. You can take a seriously damaged frame to a collision repair center, but we use a come-along and a heating torch for the more minor problems.

Check the frame first. Most of the time you find some man-made damage. Look over the frame for makeshift holes or trailer hitches. Make sure all of the flaws are repaired and then begin sandblasting. Don't be surprised if the frame takes a while to sandblast. It can take hours or even days to sandblast a frame. If the frame has deep rust pits, you might

The entire frame restoration process can be accomplished on sawhorses. You will find that two or three people are needed to safely flip it over.

However, a rotisserie only requires one person and the frame can be fixed at different angles.

want to apply an etching primer, otherwise an epoxy primer should be applied. The nice thing about sandblasting is that the steel is basically prepped. You should blow off the metal with compressed air so it is free of sand. Other than that, it's ready for primer. If you have transported the metal to and from a sandblasting shop, then it should be cleaned with wax and grease remover. Any pits can be filled with a standard body filler and then sanded with a 180-grit dual action (D/A) sander. Next, a primer/surfacer such as Spies Hecker 5110 should be applied and sanded with 500-grit wet sandpaper. The frame is then finished in semi-gloss black paint.

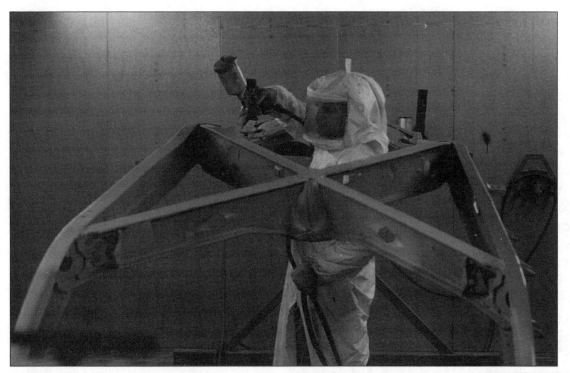

Remember what you learned in the paint chapters? This is the easiest and safest way to paint. The painter is using an outside air supply unit and a full body paint suit. He's completely isolated from the chemicals in the paint. Every nook and cranny can be easily reached when using a rotisserie.

Notice that this frame has some white lettering on its passenger side. This frame is the base of a General Motors car and most GM frames were supplied by A.O. Smith Co. You usually find a AOS number and a date on cars with A.O. Smith frames. Show cars need to have these certain details reproduced.

This color duplicates the original grease-based paint automakers used in the 1950s and 1960s. Different organizations prefer slightly altered shades of black so check with your fellow club members first. I had to experiment a little to find the right shade of black, but the finished result was roughly one part gloss black to one part flattening agent. When you find the color you want, it's a good idea to record your formula in your journal for duplication later on.

The rest of the chassis components such as the upper and lower control arms are painted the same shade as the frame, but the springs and steering linkage are different depending on the car. You should research whether these parts are natural steel or semi-gloss black. Some parts are left natural, so

The front suspension of this chassis was completed with the frame on jack stands and then elevated to sawhorses for easier assembly. The front wheel and brake assemblies can be installed and the unit lowered on two finished rims before any rear end work is even started. This way you only have to remember 50 or so parts instead of 100 (minus all of the hardware, of course). You should have realized by now that I overemphasize the memory factor. This is because I have more trouble remembering where every part goes during assembly, than I do with the actual restoration of the parts.

these components are painted a natural steel or cast iron color. The Eastwood Company sells several aerosol colors that are useful here. Some people like to then clear coat the parts for extra rust protection. I have found this process time consuming and unnecessary. If your parts are first primered with epoxy, The Eastwood Company's paint is more than enough protection. Some people might try to convince you to clear coat the sandblasted steel to obtain a more authentic look, but I strongly disagree with this method. Most of the parts I've seen done this way show oxidation within a few years. My theory is to restore the car so that it will last at least 20 years in prime condition. Obviously, you do not drive a show car every day and this counts for many of those years, but the quality of the restoration is crucial.

I have found that the front end rebuild kits available through some catalog parts suppliers tend to rust quickly, so I just send in the original parts to be plated in black zinc. These parts rarely need to be purchased new, but if yours are worn, then be sure to have them plated for rust protection. Be sure to inspect the steering linkage and tie rod ends. Once again, these parts rarely need to be purchased new, but if needed they are available from Kanter Auto Products of Boonton, N.J. Keep in mind that some catalog parts suppliers pay little attention to authenticity. They are great for hard-to-find parts for daily drivers, but their products will cause point deductions if installed on show cars. I generally get my brake pads from these suppliers and nothing else.

I always bead blast and paint my emergency brake cables natural steel color instead of buying them new. I have found most new ones to be anything but authentic in appearance.

Most differentials on collector cars are not black. Most are either red oxide or aluminum. There is a red oxide epoxy

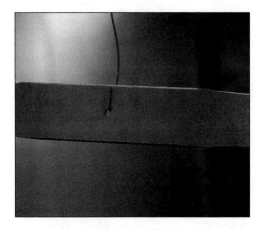

Learn to hang small- to medium-sized parts on hooks for primering and painting. If you look closely, you will see a GM stamping to the right of the hook. These stampings will add to the detail of the car and should not be filled in.

Rims sprayed with high build primers will chip and crack around the lugnuts and rim edge. Epoxy primer is the most durable primer on the market.

A finished chassis is a beautiful thing. The chassis is my favorite part on the whole car. It's both fun and motivational to restore. I once took only the chassis to a show. I knew that I wouldn't be eligible for any awards, but I thought it would be fun anyway. It turned out that I got more response and interest in the chassis than I did the finished car. People like to see what makes a car go!

primer that is close to the correct color. Depending on how picky you get, the actual red oxide shade is a little darker than what you find on the shelf. In order to get the proper shade, I mix in a small amount of green paint. Every marque can be different, so experiment with an original piece and small increments of green to find the right mix.

Painted rims have frustrated restorers for years. I have found a way to make them look beautiful. I sandblast the rim like everything else and then prime the whole rim with epoxy primer. You do not want to use build-up primer to fill pits on rims. This is because the rims endure enormous stress and frequently change shape. This can lead to paint separation. You can make a durable build-up primer out of epoxy by adding glass powder (found at fiberglass dealers) in small quantities to get a lump-free paste. Then add enough epoxy primer so it will shoot through the gun. This mixture will go on thick, like build-up primer. You will have to wet sand it with 320-grit or coarser to cut it down. Epoxy is difficult to sand as it is, but with the glass added it is almost indestructible.

New wheel bearings can be purchased from Egge Machine in Santa Fe Springs, California. There are several tire companies to choose from for the purchase of authentic looking tires. I do not have a preference. They all offer just about every kind of tire imaginable.

Well, that's the chassis restoration. The assembly should be fairly simple. You basically assemble the chassis backwards from the order that you took it apart. It takes me four months of full-time work to complete a chassis. If you work on your car only one day a week, it could take you more than two years. Time must be considered in a successful restoration. At some point you will lose interest. If your free time is limited, then you should be farming out certain tasks. For instance, contract the frame to someone else. While the frame is being restored, you can be restoring the suspension. With some careful planning, the frame and suspension will be completed at the same time, thereby cutting your restoration time in half.

Chapter 11

The Engine Compartment

The engine compartment is one of the most important parts of a restoration. It's hard to believe, but people look at the engine compartment more than any other area of the car. The next time you are at your local Saturday night hangout, watch what the other people are doing. You will probably notice that the cars with hoods up have a gathering in front and the ones with hoods down are looking a little lonely.

The engine compartment is restored in two phases. The first phase involves the restoration of the drivetrain. It is easier to install the engine, transmission, exhaust system, brake lines and fuel lines with the car body off the frame. We will start with the engine and transmission. Most restoration

Not all engine blocks are completely clean when they come back from the machine shop. If your block still has sludge buildup, then use a hand-held wire brush and some degreaser or solvent to scrape it off. It is important that all grease or oil be removed before using the die grinder and wire brush attachment. If it is not clean, the air tool will just smear the grease around and contaminate a larger area.

books spend too much time here. There are dozens of books and magazines about rebuilding engines for you to look at, so I'm going to skip the actual rebuilding process and teach you how to properly paint the engine (something all the others seem to leave out). As for transmissions, I always have a transmission shop rebuild mine. I feel that they are just too complicated.

When you are rebuilding your engine make sure that the machine shop cleans the block thoroughly. Some shops have switched to a more environmentally friendly chemical that doesn't work as well. Most of the time the blocks come back with paint or sludge still attached. The machine shops are used to this and let it slide. If you demand that it be completely clean when you drop off the block, they will know to pay a little more attention to you and your property.

I have found that both engines and transmissions can take a while to rebuild. For instance, an early 1950s Pontiac once gave me a real struggle. Most Pontiacs of this period have straight eight (inline eight-cylinder) engines that have become rather rare. It turns out that the block on this Pontiac was cracked so I purchased an additional straight eight engine from a wrecking yard. Well, this engine was also cracked, and I eventually went through a total of five blocks with no success. This was rather frustrating, but thankfully I got lucky with number six. It only takes one experience such as this to toss your whole budget right out the window, and you haven't even gotten to the paint, chrome or interior yet.

If you have a professional rebuild the engine and transmission, you can use this time to restore the chassis or body. I send all of my engines to Henderson Automotive and I send my transmissions to different shops, depending on the transmission's age and marque. I've known the people at Henderson Automotive for years and it is one of the shops that I trust. I use the time that would have been spent on the engine and transmission to restore the chassis. The idea is to have the chassis finished and waiting when they arrive.

Often, these engine/transmission professionals are not used to working on real old cars. Their experience usually runs back to the mid-1960s. If your car is older, they might not know where to get internal engine or transmission parts. Two good parts sources are Kanter Auto Parts and Egge Machine. The engine rebuilder will probably recommend hardened valve seats and stainless steel valves. These additions add to the parts cost considerably, but are well worth the money in the long run. The hardened seats and valves are required for today's unleaded gasolines.

This engine has been wire brushed clean, degreased and is ready for paint. An engine stand really comes in handy here.

The paint process for both the engine and transmission are identical, so for the rest of this chapter I will be referring mainly to the engine, but explaining both. The engine needs to be stripped before any primer can be applied. Some people like to sandblast the block, but I have always felt this is an unnecessary risk. I prefer to use a wire wheel attachment on a straight die grinder. The wire wheel will strip the block to a bright metallic finish without the risk of any internal damage from sandy grit or dust. As mentioned earlier, it is important to use safety goggles with wire brush attachments because they have a tendency to shed wires at high speeds.

The engine is then cleaned several times with a wax and grease remover. It usually takes four to six cleanings to get the metal completely free of dirt and oil. The engine and transmission are then shot with one complete coat of epoxy primer. Remember that some transmissions are aluminum and are left natural. Most transmissions are semi-gloss black or engine color. Most assembly lines would mate the engine and transmission before painting. Sometimes you find an overzealous painter has painted the entire assembly engine color. Once again, research through your club to find out which color or combination of colors is correct for your car.

If you don't know how to determine the proper engine color then obtain a catalog from Bill Hirsh. I usually order a can of paint to get the proper color and then match it to a Spies Hecker paint. This is really the secret to obtaining a long-lasting gloss on engines. Standard engine enamels have ei-

This transmission happens to be black. Notice the inspection marks dabbed across the top. The pans on the side and bottom are a natural steel color. One could argue that this is not correct, but I've seen it both ways. Sometimes transmissions were assembled after the core was painted. Always check with your club's technical advisor before you paint.

Also pictured in Chapter 5, this small parts cleaner can be useful again during the engine rebuilding phase. Most of the engine compartment components will be covered in sludge. Scrubbing the parts first will keep your bead blasting cabinet clean and free from contamination.

ther a weak catalyst or none at all. That is why they break down and fade so quickly. The engine and transmission assembly can now be mated to the chassis. Most engine mounts can be found new or revulcanized through Steele Rubber Products.

The other secret to beautiful engines lies in the body work. I tap out the dents on the engine and transmission pans, fill them with Metal-2-Metal and apply several coats of epoxy primer. The primer is wet sanded with 500 grit and painted. I also like to color sand and buff the oil pan. This gives a slightly better-than-new look that can be taboo in some clubs. You need to check with your club's rules before doing this.

The next priority is to restore and assemble what is necessary to get the engine started. I would send the carburetor to one of the carb shops advertising in *Old Cars Weekly News & Marketplace* or *Hemmings Motor News*. The exhaust manifold(s) can be sandblasted and painted with a metallic high temperature paint offered by The Eastwood Company.

There are also companies that advertise in *Old Cars Weekly News & Marketplace* or *Hemmings Motor News* that will restore your distributor, starter and generator. This is an added cost, but the advantage of using these businesses is that they have access to the various decals and tags that really make a restoration stand out. For instance, General Motors used Delco-Remy starters. These companies have the ability to reproduce the Delco-Remy tag. The original tags and decals can be a great asset at a show, and give your engine compartment much needed detail.

Egge Machine can help you with your fuel pump, oil pump and water pump. They can either send you rebuild kits or exchange your core with an original that has been rebuilt. One thing that I like about this company is that they

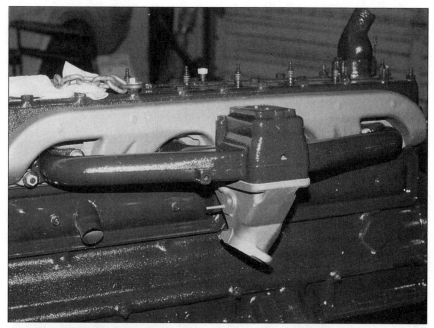

I like to use The Eastwood Company's high temp paint on exhaust manifolds. This paint will keep the manifold looking new. Most engines were painted after they were assembled. This means that both the intake and exhaust manifolds were painted engine color. However, the paint on the exhaust manifold burned off almost immediately. The end result is the exhaust manifolds oxidized before they left the factory and some clubs prefer the rusty look.

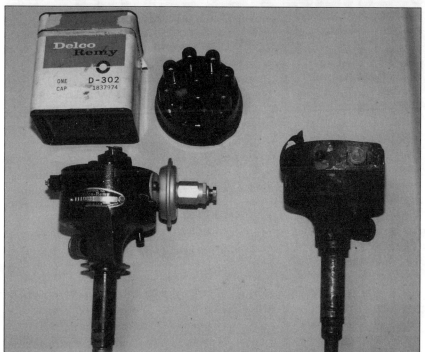

The distributor on the left has been restored with the new Delco tag. It might seem like a picky detail, but judges spend a lot of time in the engine compartment.

Your eyes don't necessarily pick out one little detail, but a highly detailed engine is pleasing to look at and stands out even 10 feet away. The first impression is critical when dealing with show cars.

It is easier to install the brake system with the body out of the way. Some master cylinders are mounted on the frame and others on the firewall. If stainless steel is used, a brand new appearance can be maintained for years.

The exhaust system can be next to impossible to install without scratching something. However, the task isn't so difficult with the body off the frame. This chassis also has the body mounts in place.

pay attention to authenticity. You won't get some overseas aftermarket part at Egge Machine.

Shock absorbers can be a little tricky. Most of the older shock absorbers were stamped with a date and some even have a special shape. For instance, most 1950s GM cars had Delco spiral shaped shocks. People look for these at shows. A bright yellow gas charged shock is a show no-no! These shocks are supposed to be semi-gloss black like almost everything else. They rarely wear out, so your originals can most likely be used or you can find them on parts cars.

Like the fuel and brake lines, I prefer a stainless exhaust system. Mild steel exhaust pipes quickly show signs of rust. The exhaust system does not have to be installed before engine start up, but your neighbors will appreciate it. Besides, you have to have it installed before the body can be lowered to the chassis anyway.

The radiator is also one of the most important components in the engine compartment. Radiators are positioned in front and are the easiest part to inspect on a vehicle. It is imperative that they be virtually flawless. When you take your original core to a radiator shop, first have the unit pressure checked. You just want to find out if the top or bottom tanks leak. Always have a new core installed. They just aren't that expensive. Tell the shop that you want to take the top tank home before they solder the unit back together. Old radiators are almost always brass and are easily dented. You can place the tank on a dolly and gently tap out the dents from the back side. Then bring it back to the radiator shop to have the unit soldered.

Next cover the radiator's core fins with cardboard and duct tape. Lightly sandblast the tanks and sides to remove any rust and oxidation. Epoxy the entire radiator and apply several coats to the top tank. Radiators get hot and expand and contract rather severely so do not ever put body filler on the dents. I'm going to reveal the secret to beautiful radiators for the first time (not even the Pontiac club members know this one, and believe me they've asked). The secret is J.B. Weld! Mix up the weld and spread it on the low spots, just like body filler. It usually takes a day to dry and I use a six-inch block with 120-grit dry sandpaper to block the weld smooth. Sometimes you have to repeat the procedure to properly fill all of the low spots. When you are satisfied, apply several more coats of epoxy primer. The radiator is now ready to be wet sanded with 400 grit and painted. Radiators are usually painted gloss black. Don't forget to first clean the surface with wax and grease remover. I also like to gently wet sand the top tank with 1500 grit and compound (liquid for polishing paint) the paint to get a deep, glossy shine. There is a chapter later in the book that will explain this process thoroughly.

You are ready to test run the engine. Triple check that the engine and transmission have oil. I know it sounds silly, but people have a tendency to overlook the obvious. I would not install the driveshaft just yet. This is just a safety precaution. In fact, I would not install the driveshaft until the car was almost finished. Many cars have the brake booster on the firewall, so chances are you do not have any brakes at this point in the restoration. The chassis is fairly light, too. When your engine starts, with driveshaft installed and no brakes your chassis (and hard work) could launch down the street like a rocket. This can be fairly amusing, but only if it's not your chassis!

Your engine rebuild books should have a section devoted to initial start-up, so be sure to first cross reference those

A dent free radiator is a must. The trick lies in performing body work to the top tank. However, normal body fillers will crack with the heat and expansion normally associated with radiators. The secret to beautiful radiators is revealed in the text!

Some clubs prefer semi-gloss black to gloss. If this is the case, then try The Eastwood Company's radiator black aerosol. (Photo courtesy of The Eastwood Company)

An engine hoist and a floor jack are necessary tools for this procedure. Use the jack to bring the transmission to the engine, not the other way around. Most engine hoists are just not that accurate.

The engine assembly is ready to be lowered to the frame. Hopefully you ordered the engine mounts ahead of time. A Phillips head screwdriver can be used to line up the mounts from underneath.

books. I like to set the timing at this time, too. You will find that the engine is easy to work on without any fenders or hood in the way. Your first engine start-up is a real accomplishment. I still become excited every time I do it. Invite your friends over and celebrate -- you deserve it!

The steering box is optional depending on the method of body removal used. If you used an engine hoist and sawhorses, the steering column will only get in the way during assembly. Spend all of your time restoring the components necessary for engine start-up. Only switch to body restoration if you get stuck waiting on parts.

It's party time!

Chapter 12

Rust Repair

Cars with vinyl tops usually have some degree of rust. Surface rust can usually be found all over the top of the roof. This is due to moisture settling under the vinyl and being trapped there for long periods of time. Even more damage can be found around the back windows of vinyl tops. It's common to find moderate rust at the bottom edge of the rear window.

Those of you with steel body cars will have some rust. Rust is normal and all steel cars have some rust or oxidation regardless of their age. Even brand new cars have some degree of rust somewhere. It is the degree and location of the rust that is important.

The most mild form of rust is surface rust. It can usually be found under stainless trim and beneath gaskets. This form of rust might have some pitting but has not yet eaten through to form a hole. It is repaired by mechanically stripping off the oxidation to expose bright steel. Sandblasters are the tool of choice, but there are some circumstances where they should not be used. Those of you who are not performing a complete restoration should shy away from sandblasting. If your trim or glass is still installed, remember that sandblasting is indiscriminate and will quickly damage these items. The sand will do a number on your interior and engine compartment. When dealing with delicate areas, I prefer to use a wire brush or pen tip grinder extension on a straight die grinder to work loose the rust. I then clean the surface and apply an etching primer. Next, I apply a coat of epoxy primer and fill the pits with body filler. One more coat of epoxy, and you will forget the rust was ever there.

The next form of rust is the most common and resembles Swiss cheese. This level of rust is usually found around the lower perimeter of the body. Check the firewall, rocker panels and trunk valence panel for spotted rust and holes. There are three ways to fix this kind of rust, but the steel should be sandblasted or stripped with the die grinder before you decide which. Most of the time, rust damage becomes more clear when the steel has been completely stripped. Rust usually flakes up and covers the true extent of the damage. This is why you have to strip the steel before any decisions can be made.

The first method uses a Mig welder. If the holes are small, you simply weld them. The welder usually burns back the metal some, but there are ways to control this. Most people turn down the welder's voltage or heat setting. This reduces the strength of the weld and can cause it to crack or fall out in time. The best way is to use short bursts of voltage around the edge of the hole. Be sure to cool down the steel with compressed air between welds. The idea behind this technique is to build up an edge and strengthen the border of the rust hole. Once the edges have been beefed up, you will find that the hole is fairly easy to weld. Only the holes need to be welded. The high spots of the weld are ground off and the pits are filled like before. Remember that any heat buildup will severely warp the steel.

Another option is to fill small holes with fiberglass or fiber body filler. The area is then sanded flush with the rest of the panel and primered with epoxy primer. It is a good idea to primer the stripped steel before any filler is used. I use this technique on all of the parts and body areas that have no real structural purpose. This technique can save a lot of time on minor parts such as splash pans, bumper filler pans and fender skirts. This technique can also be used at the bottom of firewalls and rocker panels if the rust is not too severe.

For larger holes or holes that are found in structurally important areas, you can cut the rusted area with a cutoff wheel. The cutout can then be used as a pattern on a piece of fresh steel. The new piece can be trimmed to fit and butt welded into the hole. You might have to hammer and dolly

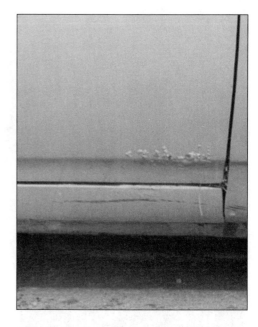

The bottom of this door has some bubbled paint. This is a sign of rust. Flaky rust is under the paint, and it usually has rusted through. This is the tricky thing about rust. The true nature of the damage doesn't reveal itself until the steel has been completely stripped.

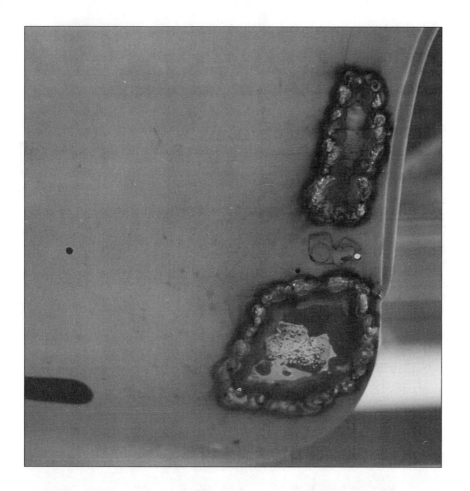

The bottom of wheel wells is another common place for rust. If the holes are larger than a half inch, it is better to weld in some fresh steel. The damaged area was first cut out and new steel was trimmed to fit. Getting the proper curvature on a small area such as this is easy. Start with two tack welds at the top and at each side of the hole. The new metal will be sticking out at the bottom. Using a screwdriver, push the metal in and place two more tack welds approximately one-half inch below the top welds. Repeat this process all of the way down. Be sure the new metal is flush with the panel at the location of each weld. If a mistake is made, break the tack weld loose and try again.

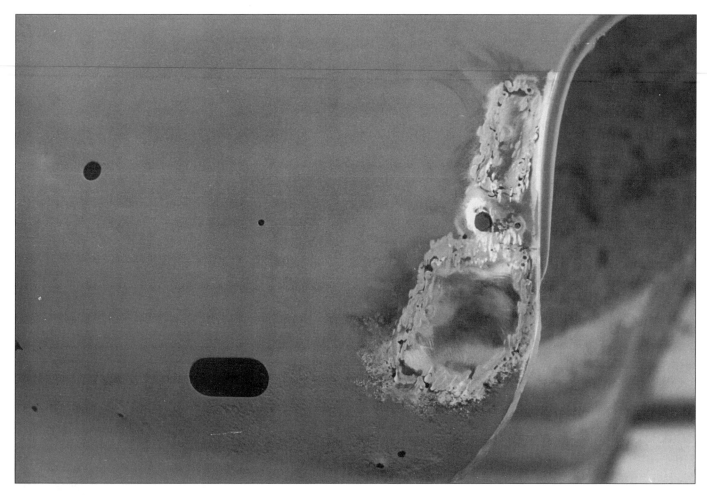

Once you are satisfied with the shape of the spliced-in metal, carefully weld the rest of the piece. Be sure only to weld one dot at a time and to cool the area with compressed air. When the weld is complete, grind the welds flush with the rest of the panel. The area is now ready for primer and body filler. This kind of minor repair is excellent for building welding skills.

the steel to get the correct body curvature. The excess weld is ground flush and body filler can be used to fill the imperfections. Try to use the same gauge steel for replacement panels and, once again, do not forget to keep the area cool.

The next level of rust is called severe or "Why the hell did I buy this car?" rust. Now you know why I spent the first three chapters teaching you how to find and purchase the right car. Repairing large rust holes properly can be very labor intensive. Large rust holes can add $2,000 to $20,000 to the price of a restoration. It is always better to spend a little extra and get a car without extensive rust. However, these days it is getting difficult to find convertibles without severe rust problems. You might not have much to choose from. In this case, you will be faced with some panel replacement work. Severe rust damage requires the replacement of the damaged area with a new panel. Damage to this extent should never be filled or repaired with fiberglass.

So, where do you find replacement panels? Those of you with 1960s and newer cars, Fords or Chevys are in luck. Most of the lower sheet metal on these cars is being reproduced. Check in *Old Cars Weekly News & Marketplace* or *Hemmings Motor News* for companies that stamp sheet metal for your

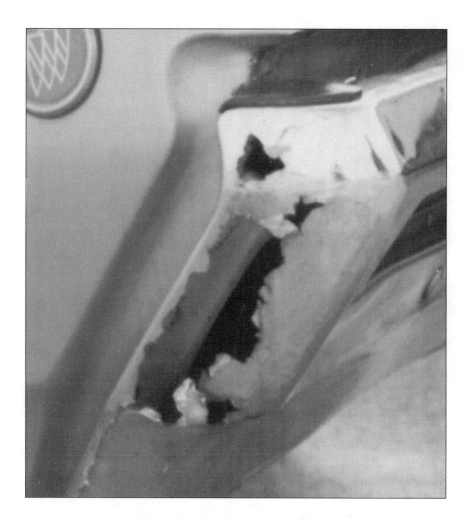

With enough effort, this bumper could be repaired. The problem is that you will spend weeks fooling around with a $200 bumper. The time would be better spent blocking your body straight and preparing it for paint.

marque and year. Those of you with the more uncommon marques will have to find the panels on parts cars. I prefer parts car panels to reproductions anyway. Many of the new panels don't fit correctly or don't have the original stamping on them.

It is usually faster and cheaper to replace a whole component than it is to repair one. This is due more to labor than the cost of parts. Let's take a door, for example. Convertible and hardtop doors are getting expensive, but let's say due to rust your door is missing an inch all the way across the bottom. A "rust free" door in a salvage yard in Arizona will cost you $400 including shipping. Your first instinct is to repair the door, but the door will take 20 hours to return it to excellent condition. Remember, always rate your time at $25 per hour. Repairing the door costs you $500 so you lose $100 by not purchasing a fresh door. You also have to consider that the 20 hours of time can be spent doing something else. Use the time waiting for the fresh door to arrive to do the body work on a fender. Now you have a door and a fender in the same time that you would have one door.

There are a lot of people that *disagree* with this strategy. Obviously, if you don't have $400 there is a problem with

Rear trunk panels are a common place for rust. The rusty panel has been cut away with a cutoff wheel and a plasma cutter. Plasma cutters are wonderful tools, but I can't recommend the $1,000-$2,000 cost for those of you who do not plan on restoring several cars. Cutoff wheels are far more economical.

The inside is then sandblasted to determine the true extent of the damage. Notice how much easier it is to see the rust damage after the area has been cleaned.

this logic. Again, I cannot stress enough the importance of time in a restoration. Through the course of the 5,000 parts, if you can shave 20 percent of the hours involved, you have just saved yourself a year or more!

I also realize that some will argue that part replacement means the car is no longer "original." I see their point, but only to the point that if you restore the car in any way it loses its originality. Why make things more difficult for yourself when you can find a better part?

Floor pan replacement is the most common repair. The concept is fairly simple, but I highly recommend hiring a professional for all kinds of panel replacement. Although it sounds simple on paper, it is one of the most difficult aspects of auto restoration. A high degree of skill is needed to complete the task.

The idea here is to cut out the old panel and weld in a new one. It doesn't sound too difficult, but where you make your cut is extremely important and requires skill. A cut in the wrong place can make a car unrestorable. Remember that you only want to cut the floor pan and not the rocker edges or any of the braces under the floor. This means that your tool selection is rather limited. *Never* use a cutting torch to cut a panel! I have found that a cutoff wheel attachment on a die grinder is the best tool. Next you must determine whether or not you are going to replace the entire panel or just make a spot repair. This is determined by the size of the

I like to repair unseen areas with Kitty Hair body filler, and shoot primer on the inside for rust protection. Next, a fresh panel is cut out of a donor car and trimmed to fit. Notice that the gaps at the right and left are too big. This is because the corners are going to be replaced as well. That decision was made after the steel was sandblasted. Once clean, it became evident that the corners would have to be replaced as well.

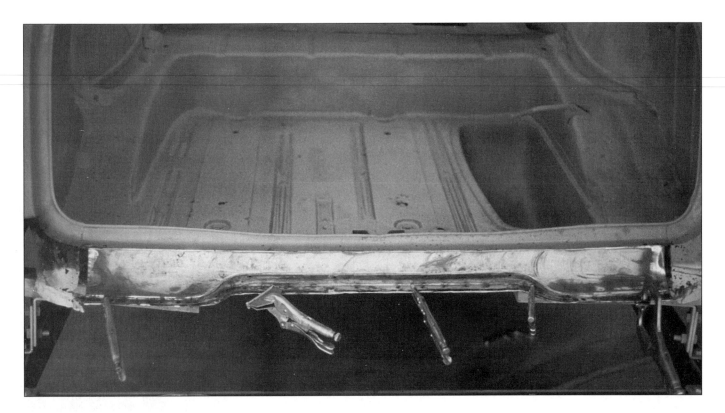

The donor panel is centered and tack welded into place. Locking pliers can be used to hold the panel still during welding. Notice that the left corner has been cut away. Once removed, even more rust problems were found. Sometimes rust repair can be like chasing a pot of gold at the end of a rainbow. This car should not have been purchased. At this point, we have already spent more in rust repair costs than the owner saved by buying the less expensive car available at the time of purchase. I see so many people make this mistake, and that's why I spent so much time at the beginning of this book teaching you how to find the right car for restoration.

hole. If the hole is larger than a basketball, you should replace the entire panel.

Spot repair is described towards the beginning of this chapter and is not difficult, but entire panel replacement is another thing. The panels are spot welded together to form the car's body. These spot welds have to be separated in order to remove the panel. A cutoff wheel is used to grind down the spot weld. When the spot weld is loose, you will see a circular crack or shadow around the weld. This process must be repeated for every spot weld around the panel. It is time consuming and requires patience. Be careful not to cut into the brace or lower panel edge.

The panel, in this case the floor pan, can now be removed. The replacement panel is then set into place to determine the fit. New panels rarely fit the first time. They are usually larger than the original and will require their edges to be trimmed for a proper fit. Quarter-inch holes should be punched or drilled around the edge of the new panel. These should approximate the number and location of the original spot welds. The panel is set into place and welded at each hole. When the hole is filled in with steel, you know the weld is finished.

If your car requires a great deal of panel replacement, you should consider purchasing a book on welding. Welding is not something you know how to do at birth. It takes a good deal of practice and patience to do properly.

The corners are in place and the welds have been ground flush with the rest of the body. The steel needs to be stripped and primered. All that remains is a little body filler at the seams to get a smooth finish. The repair is complete, and a rust free trunk panel has been achieved. The problem is that the floor pans need to be replaced in this body and a small fortune has already been spent. If the best convertible you can find is like this one, than be prepared to spend a lot of time in the rust repair mode.

This is what a proper floor pan removal should look like. Notice that the braces under the floor are untouched (see arrow). An inexperienced restorer will just take a cutting torch and start cutting away. You know better now! Most of those braces are not being reproduced, so be careful. Take your time and treat them with respect.

Chapter 13

Dent Removal and Body Work

A quarter panel can be a real problem. This panel should be replaced, but most of the time you don't have this option because replacement quarter panels are rare. In these cases, you are forced to straighten out the panel, and you can spend weeks doing it.

Once your car has been stripped to bare steel, removed of all rust and primered with epoxy primer, all dents and minor collision damage must be repaired. I will not cover major collision repair in this book due to the complexity and expense of the equipment involved. Once again, I cannot stress how important it is to purchase the right car for restoration. If you made the purchase before obtaining this book and have discovered major collision damage, then you should take the car to a professional collision repair center for straightening. However, I would seriously consider dumping the project altogether. You will spend far more repairing

major collision damage than what an additional car body and frame will cost.

Most cars, however, just have minor door and fender dings. These are fairly easy to repair. The dent should first be tapped or pulled as close to level as possible. There will be some sheet metal that can be accessed from both sides. For example, fenders and hoods can be accessed on the outside as well as inside surfaces. A hammer and dolly can be used to tap out dents in such areas. The idea here is to locate the dent and tap it out from the lowest side. The outside surface should be backed up with a dolly. The dolly's primary purpose is to prevent you from tapping the dent too far and creating a high spot instead of a dent. The goal is to hammer the dent outward so the steel is close to, but not quite at the surface. Once again, this is where my method is slightly different from others. I've seen people become obsessed with

It is sometimes impossible to tap out dents by yourself. Try to work out all of the dents you can and then recruit a friend to hold the dolly in the hard-to-reach areas.

A body rotisserie is a necessity for those of you with sedans. Don't try to crawl up on the roof to work out dents. You will end up creating your own problems if you do.

I pick up sedans by lifting on a chain that is bolted to either side of the floor. You won't be able to lift at the exact center of gravity, but try to set it up so that one man can easily steady the body.

the idea of a "no Bondo" car. It takes four or five times longer to tap out a dent to the point where it can be finished out with primer/surfacer. It's great to brag about "no Bondo," but these people will be in the dent removal phase when they could be in the painting phase if they would just get the dent close and use body filler to finish the job.

Remember that Bondo is a brand name. There are many different grades and brands of body filler. Personally, I do not use Bondo, but I don't think there is anything wrong with the product. All polyester fillers are roughly the same. The real problem with Bondo is that it is sold in parts stores and almost every shade tree, want-to-be body man uses it. All body fillers will fail if they are not used properly. Polyester products absorb water. This is why you never wet sand body filler. You should never store a car in the body work phase outside. Even humidity will damage polyester products.

You want to go through the body filler application process as quickly as possible. If the car will be sitting for long periods of time, be sure to apply a coat of epoxy or urethane primer/surfacer for protection from moisture. Finally, *never* apply body filler over rust and always clean the surface between each coat.

The other method of dent removal involves a dent puller. The most commonly used dent puller is called a spot weld dent puller. This tool welds a small pin to the low part of the dent. Next, a special slide hammer grabs the pin and pulls out the dent. This tool is similar to the old-fashioned slide

Once the body is up, roll the jig underneath and bolt it to the floor mounts.

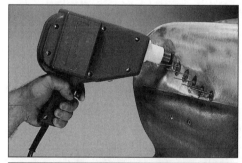

The Eastwood Company offers a nice spot weld dent pulling kit. Copper pins are welded to the surface, but try not to apply heat for more than one second intervals. Long bursts have a tendency to wear out the gun prematurely. (Photo courtesy of The Eastwood Company)

A special slide hammer attaches itself to the pins. When you are finished, all you have to do is grind the pin flush with the rest of the steel. (Photo courtesy of The Eastwood Company)

It is real easy to hurt yourself with a slide hammer. Be sure that you don't let any portion of your hand get in between the weight and the stop on the slide. This is one of the few times in auto restoration where you know you've made a mistake immediately! Ouch! (Photo courtesy of The Eastwood Company)

hammers. The problem with the old dent pullers is you must first drill a series of holes in the side of the panel. The old slide hammers had a screw at the tip, which threaded into the hole. The slide hammers often stripped out the screw in stubborn dents, leaving you with quarter-inch holes all over the panel. However, spot weld dent pullers do not damage the panel in this way. After the dent has been pulled, simply cut or grind off the pins and you are through.

Once the dents have been removed, the gross body work phase can begin. This simply entails the filling of dents and obvious low spots with body filler and quickly grinding it flush with the rest of the panel. It is important to always wipe the area clean using wax and grease remover before any filler is applied. You always see people in magazines applying coats of body filler, shaping it with a cheese grater file and then blocking it smooth. This is not necessary. Remember that this is the gross body work phase. I apply the filler, wait 20 minutes or so for it to harden and then I use the seven-inch electric grinder with a 40-grit sanding disc to power sand away the excess filler. This is the same setup I described in the paint stripping phase of this book. It is best to then lightly sand these areas with an 80-grit dual action (D/A) sander to remove the deep scratches created by the 40-grit disc. This process should take less than one day.

Next comes what is probably the most tedious phase in auto restoration -- blocking. I will first describe the process and then I will tell you why you should do this yourself and not hire a professional. First, picture the cross-section of

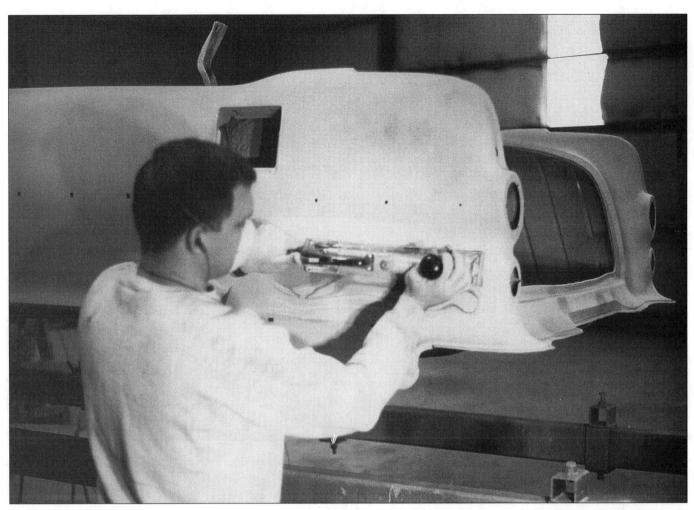

your car body's surface. At this point, the surface will look wavy like the surface of the ocean. The goal of blocking is to level the panel so that it will reflect smooth, crisp images after it has been painted. This is one of the secrets of a beautiful paint job, and few people know how to do it properly.

Most paint manufacturers offer a spray polyester product. This is a liquid body filler that can be thinned down and sprayed onto the body surface with a primer gun. If you cannot find one locally, The Eastwood Company offers a fine spray polyester called Feather Fill. Feather Fill has caused some problems, but once again, it is not the product's fault. Because some people do not have access to the proper polyester reducers, they have been using lacquer thinner instead. This is a big no-no. Be sure to read the label and follow the instructions. If you do not have access to a well-stocked paint distributor, call The Eastwood Company or Evercoat to locate the proper reducer for the product.

After several coats of spray polyester have been applied, apply a guide coat to the surface. A guide coat is nothing more than a thin or speckled layer of dark coloring. Most people use black spray paint. Mist on the paint and let it dry.

I like to start out with 80 grit on an air-powered file sander. This is a fast and aggressive process, so care needs to be used around curvy and flared areas. This tool has a tendency to dig into flared areas (like most wheel well edges) and leave a thin gouge. Be sure to remain at least one inch away from curved and flared areas when using this tool.

3M soft foam hand pads make perfect blocks for curvy areas such as those around the taillight housings.

Use the guide coat to determine where more filler or spray polyester needs to be applied through the blocking process.

There are several tools needed for this task to be successful. I use an array of sanding blocks. File paper is a dry sanding paper that comes in continuous rolls and in a standard width. You just pull and tear off the length desired. This should tell you that most of the blocks you buy are already made for this width. However, I have not found any commercial blocks long enough to be of any use. I go to a hobby shop and buy three-foot lengths of balsa wood and break these down to other lengths. I use 36-, 24- and 18-inch blocks. How do you know which one to use? This mainly comes from experience, but try to find one that is a foot short on either side from the flat panel length. This does not mean the whole panel length, but only the flat, sandable portion of the panel. Soft foam blocks will be used on curvy areas such as the tops of fins or around taillight housings. There will also be areas that need to be blocked, but the standard width blocks will be too wide. You usually have these situations at the tops of panels or along the rockers. A narrow block can be manufactured from a paint stick and some foam board in-

sulation. Cut the insulation board so that you have a piece the same size as the paint stick. Then glue the foam to one side of the stick. You now have the perfect rocker panel block.

File paper can be purchased in many grits. I usually start with 80 or 120 grit. Sight down the length of the board and determine if the board is straight. Most blocks are not. I actually prefer a block that has a slight bow to it. Place the board on a flat surface so that the two ends are pointing or lifting up. From now on I will be referring to the down side as the inside of the block and the top side as the outside. The sandpaper will have a sticky surface that will be applied to the inside of the block. Now place the sandpaper side of the board to the surface of the car. The ends should be slightly lifting up. Next, hold the block just slightly in from the two ends and press the block so that the ends are touching the surface of the car. This is all the pressure that is needed to block sand a car. Most people use too much pressure and end up sanding in some of the problems they are trying to fix.

Air tools can only take you so far. After one or two blocking procedures, the car body requires a human touch. On long panels such as this one, you will have to use a long block. The longest in my inventory is three feet.

The guide coat does not have to be a full, solid coat. A light mist of spray paint is all that is needed.

This is where the guide coats come in. You block the surface in an angular fashion. In other words, block in long strokes from your bottom left to the upper right. Never block straight up and down or side-to-side. This will leave gouges or lines in the panel. As you are blocking, notice that the spray polyester will begin to fall off in some places and not in others. Take several passes and then switch directions (your bottom right to your upper left). Be sure to move around the panel and don't try to sand all of the guide coat in one pass. Repeat the sanding process until metal begins to show. If some metal shows fairly quickly, then you have a high spot.

High spots are cured by gently tapping them with a body pick hammer. Always tap in a little at a time. Continue blocking until large areas of metal appear. The dark areas will be the low spots and a judgment call has to be made as to whether these will be filled with body filler or more spray polyester. Generally, if you rub your hand across it and feel it, the area is low enough to warrant more body filler. On the first blocking, it is likely that more filler will be needed. Once dry, the filler is blocked so that it is smooth and flush with the surrounding area. I refer to this as blocking out. There might be areas where more filler is needed. These become evident when the filler has been blocked out and some areas

Notice the different colors after you have sanded. You have low spots where the guide coat remains untouched and high spots where metal shows through.

appear to be untouched. Once again, these are more low spots and they are to be filled and blocked out. You might have to repeat this process several times. It is important that the surface be cleaned with wax and grease remover between every application.

Once the panel is cleaned and reshot with spray polyester, the entire guide coat and blocking process is then repeated. Once again, watch the panel as you sand. The low spots should be getting smaller and shallower. You should not have to use any more body filler at this point. Through this whole initial blocking phase, I like to use an air file sander. This tool is approximately 18 inches long and costs around $250. I do not consider this tool a necessity, but it will speed up these initial blocking steps tenfold. Repeat this process until the panel no longer has any remaining low spots or guide coat. The initial blocking phase is then complete.

At this point, I would apply one more coat of spray polyester, but this time I would use the longer, hand-held blocks. Notice that more low spots will appear. This is because the air sander is not precise. The longer the block, the straighter the panel will become. It is likely that you will have to repeat the blocking process several times.

The process isn't over, though. Now four or five coats of high build surfacer is applied. In the Spies Hecker system, 5110 is the primer/surfacer of choice. Ask your paint dealer what high build surfacer is recommended in your paint sys-

Use your judgment to decide whether the low spots require body filler or more spray polyester. Experience will tell you how much spray polyester will fill. When you are finished sanding, the panel will have a tiger-striped appearance. The panel is cleaned and reshot with spray polyester. This process is repeated until you are satisfied that the panel is straight.

tem. Once the surfacer is dry, the blocking procedure is repeated. However, this time you use a 200+ sanding grit. I use 220-grit file paper in this step. This procedure is repeated until you are satisfied that the panel is straight.

It helps to lightly wet down the surface and look at the reflections in the surface. Pick an object in the reflection and position yourself so that you are sighting down the panel. Next, slowly move from left to right while fixating on that object. The reflection should not flutter or look wavy. If it does, then you know the panel is not finished. It generally takes me two months, or 320 hours of work to block a car to perfection. This is why you do this yourself. First of all, no body shop is going to spend two months blocking your car; even if you do find someone that is competent at it, you will be paying them $40-$50 per hour. That adds up to more than $10,000 in the blocking phase alone (plus chemicals)! Trust me, it isn't difficult. It is just unbelievably tedious and time consuming.

Once the car has been blocked for the final time, apply one more coat of surfacer and wet sand it with 500-grit wet/dry paper. The car is now ready for paint.

Chapter 14

Floor Restoration

It is usually easier to restore the underside of the floor before the body is painted. The body should be lifted or turned on its side for easier access. The floor is then sandblasted and primered in epoxy primer. The small rust pits can then be filled with body filler. Body work on the underside of the car does not have to be as precise as the outside panels, so just sand the filler with an 80-grit D/A sander. Clean the floor with wax and grease remover and layer the sanded areas with a few coats of primer/surfacer. The surfaced areas should be sanded smooth with 500-grit wet sand paper so there is no 80-grit sanding scratches visible.

It takes some time to sandblast the underside of the floor. A rotisserie is nice, but if one is not available, the body can be set on sawhorses such as this one.

Notice that the black undercoating is sprayed around the perimeter of the body. The rear wheel wells are completely coated and the body color overspray is between the primer and the undercoating.

Next, some research must be done. Most car bodies were either left in red oxide primer or shot semi-flat black underneath. Semi-flat black is usually found underneath cars from the 1960s and 1970s. These cars are shot with flat or semi-flat black paint. Most of the 1950s cars were left in red-oxide primer. You can use a red-oxide colored epoxy primer if your car is this color. Your car might be undercoated underneath. This was generally offered from the dealerships, but most judges will take off points if you try to duplicate the process. This is because some people have been using undercoating to hide poor workmanship underneath the car. If you are not interested in points judging, it is far easier to undercoat the entire floor and be done with it.

For those of you interested in points judging, keep in mind that the factory did not mask off the car's floor prior to painting. This means that the floor should have body color overspray around the perimeter of the body's underside. The factories then undercoated the seams around the perimeter of the floor as well as the seam found above the rear axle. Some factories also undercoated the transmission tunnel of

Sawhorses will work, but it means that you will be crawling around under a body that can weigh more than 1,000 pounds. It's a good idea to have extra sawhorses for safety purposes. Position these sawhorses near the load bearing sawhorses. This is your backup should a sawhorse fail.

the floor for noise reduction. All points-judged cars should have this process repeated.

This procedure can be done before or after the body work phase -- it really doesn't matter. What's important to remember is that you should mask off the entire floor so that primer, paint and compound doesn't contaminate the finished floor.

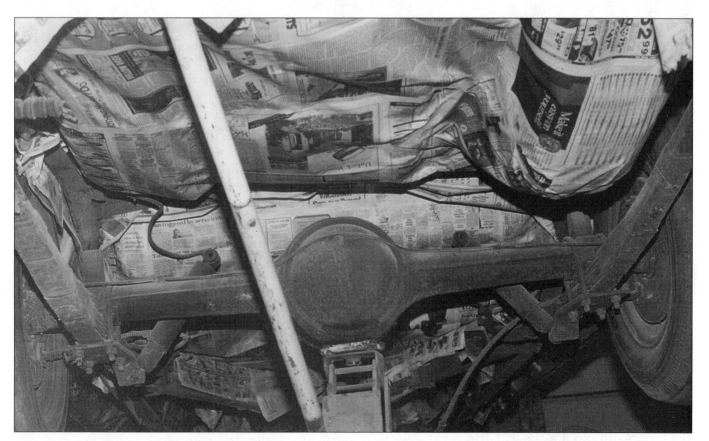

We masked off this floor with newspaper. Most people today use plastic sheet. Large rolls of plastic are available from your local paint supplier.

Chapter 15

Applying and Compounding Paint

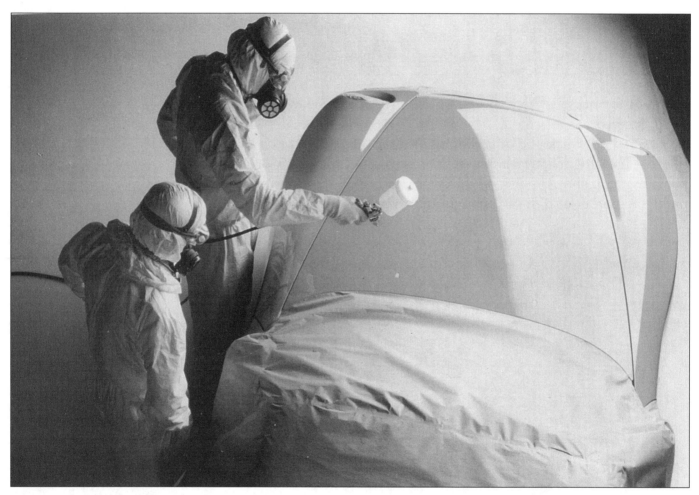

These painters are wrapped up tight. Many of you have not seen anything like this because the older, obsolete restoration books showed people painting with lacquer. Forget about lacquer, it's already illegal in most states and is on the fast track to obsolescence in the others. (Photo courtesy of The Eastwood Company)

Painting and buffing can be two of the most difficult techniques to learn in auto restoration. It takes time and patience to learn the necessary skills. If this is your first restoration, do not attempt to paint your car's body. It took me more than two years of full-time work to learn how to paint. After my apprenticeship, I switched paint suppliers and spent more than a year relearning what I thought I already knew. Every manufacturer's paint is different, so it takes time to learn how to properly apply a new paint. This is why most professionals stay with one manufacturer or brand name. In fact, when painters leave a body shop, they usually only apply for work at shops that display their brand of choice. Switching around could hamper their skills and damage their careers.

In addition to skill, the new urethane paints require a substantial investment in equipment. Urethane enamels dry slowly in comparison to lacquers. This means the time frame for the paint to attract dust is much greater and a cleaner paint environment is needed to be successful. Some form of paint booth will be needed. I've seen everything from a garage with a box fan to downdraft booths costing more than $100,000. I received most of my advanced training at the Spies Hecker training center in Dallas. Their paint booth had a fireproof storage area and explosion-proof light fixtures. This is because paint booths have a nasty habit of catching on fire. If you're bored one day and want to see people scramble, just walk into a paint booth with a lit cigarette. I'm kidding of course, but most people do not realize that a hovering paint cloud is an explosion waiting to happen.

There are also hazards other than fire. Urethane paints have highly toxic additives in their catalysts, which should not be inhaled. This is why professional painters wear a full body suit with an outside air supply. These setups cost about $1,000. The old-fashioned paint guns are now illegal. That's right! When you stand in front of your garage with an old paint gun shooting parts, you are breaking the law. All it takes is one complaint from a neighbor to your state's environmental board and you are in big trouble.

To be honest, there is no difference between shooting paint in a booth or out in the open. The same amount of solvent is exposed to the environment. Not all environmental laws make sense. You are now required to use a HVLP (high-volume low-

As pointed out in an earlier chapter, safety gear is essential. Urethane paints require the use of a full body suit to protect you from harmful vapors. (Photo courtesy of The Eastwood Company)

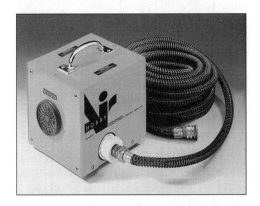

An outside air supply unit is used to pump fresh air into the suit. (Photo courtesy of The Eastwood Company)

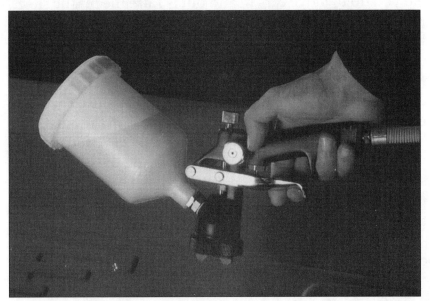

HVLP guns are one of the good things that have come as a result of the environmental movement. They use far less paint and produce almost no overspray. (Photo courtesy of The Eastwood Company)

Semi-gloss/flat colors can be shot with a normal paint gun or sprayed with an aerosol. I highly recommend aerosols. They are fast and easy to use. Best of all, there is nothing to clean when you are done. (Photo courtesy of The Eastwood Company)

It is always best to hang small parts for painting. If you set the parts down, the paint will make the parts stick to whatever surface they are on. (Photo courtesy of The Eastwood Company)

pressure) gun. This is one law that does make sense. There is a big difference between what HVLP guns release when compared to the old suction-fed guns. Go ahead and buy a HVLP gun. You will be legal and it will pay for itself through material savings in a short time.

A vehicle is composed mainly of small parts that can be painted at home. At least 50 percent of the vehicle's painted surface is painted semi-flat or semi-gloss black. These finishes do not require the same precision as the outside body panels. Therefore, chassis and engine compartment pieces make good warm-up parts for beginning painters. Refer to Chapters 10 and 11 for instruction on how to paint chassis components. Most of the engine compartment is no different. All of the inner fender wells, brackets and pulleys are painted this way. I would recommend that the highly visible components such as the inner fender wells and upper engine brackets receive extra attention. I see to it that the most visible engine compartment pieces are virtually flawless before painting. If this means more coats of surfacer and more wet sanding with 500 grit, so be it. I also like to use slightly glossier shades of semi-gloss black on these types of parts. This technique, along with the appropriate decals, will add detail to your engine compartment.

The rest of this chapter will be for those of you who want to take on the challenge of painting your car's body. You will first need a painting environment, so I would like to share with you one of the most creative solutions to this problem that I've encountered. A friend of mine built a booth in his garage by erecting a large wooden box frame and stapling plastic sheet to form the ceiling and walls. A cutout at one end houses one or more sticky air filters (these can be purchased at your local paint dealer). The opposite end has a cutout with a box fan in it. The booth has no doors. All you do to move cars in and out is raise the plastic sheet. Normal lights are used on the outside of the plastic and I believe he is using just a common box fan for exhaust. Even though he has experienced no problems, an explosion-proof fan is a *necessity*. The most common cause of booth fires comes from a spark emitted by an electric motor. Most fire codes now require that the actual motor be on the outside of the exhaust duct with a belt that turns the fan inside.

Applying paint can be a little tricky. You must first make sure that the surface and environment are clean. Most people first sweep out and wet their booth floors. Then the surface is blown repeatedly with compressed air. Next, the surface to be painted is cleaned with wax and grease remover and wiped with a tack rag to remove lint.

All kinds of tricks are used to obtain detail in an engine compartment. It is a mistake to paint all of the parts in your engine compartment one shade of semi-gloss black. This tends to drown out the engine compartment and give it a monochromatic look. Remember that the auto manufacturers didn't paint the individual components under the hood. The parts were purchased from other companies, such as AC Delco, and were painted before they were shipped. Therefore all of the parts under the hood should be different shades of semi-flat and semi-gloss black.

You generally find all kinds of instructions on cars, too. I like to look at parts cars to research what and where these instructions were located. The more authentic the detail the better.

Some additional steps might be necessary before paint. A coat of 3M brushable seam sealer is applied to the seams of this firewall to mimic its original appearance.

All paint manufacturers will put mixing instructions on their cans, but I recommend that you take their painter's class to learn any quirks or tricks that are relevant to that specific company. I can tell you that the number of coats has nothing to do with the quality of a paint job. *This is an ongoing myth.* A single coat can mean a lot of different things. I can mist a coat or pull the trigger and move so slowly that a run will form. Either of these can be accomplished in a single pass or coat. What you really want to measure is film thickness. If the thickness is too thin, you will polish through in the compounding phase, but thicker is not always better. I cringe every time I'm at a car show and hear someone brag about his "20 coats of paint." If the film thickness is too great, the stress of the drying process will cause the paint to actually lift off or crack as time goes by. I never say anything to these braggarts, though. You will find quite a few of the species *Expertus Jackassus* at car shows and I have learned it is better to leave them alone. They will not believe any of your advice anyway.

Now let's apply some paint. First, apply a tack coat. I refer to this coat as a half coat. You apply the tack coat by misting

the paint onto the surface. A tack is not a coverage coat and you should be able to see through it. Then you should wait approximately five minutes for the solvents to flash off. This time should be doubled for temperatures under 60 degrees Fahrenheit. The second coat should be one full coat. This is tricky to apply, but it is why professional paint booths have so many lights. You apply the paint while you are looking at the reflection of a light on the surface. The best way to do this is to apply multiple light coats to build up one wet coat. These coats must be applied quickly so the surface stays wet. The whole time, you should be studying the reflection. You will notice that the surface starts out rough and gets increasingly slick. Always start at the top of the panel and overlap the coats as you work your way down.

Once the entire painted surface looks wet, stop and take a five minute or longer break. After you have allowed the solvents to flash off, repeat the whole process again. I call this entire process two-and-a-half coats. The number of coats doesn't sound impressive, but I usually apply close to a quart of paint on just one 1950s or 1960s vintage fender. I have found that I don't get runs when I build up several dry, light coats to obtain a glossy coat as opposed to trying for glossy on the first pass. I know this whole process sounds confusing on paper,

Bright light is a must in your painting environment. Study the light's reflection on the surface as you apply the paint. You can actually see the surface get wet. The trick to painting properly is to apply the minimum amount of paint to get a wet, glossy appearance.

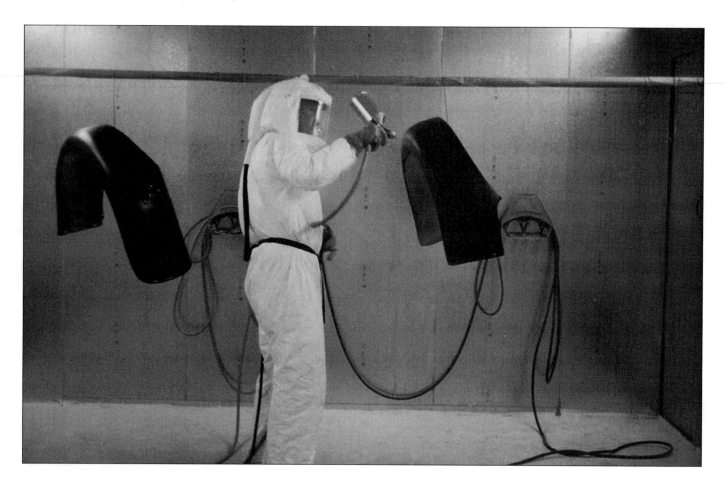

Start with just a few pieces. Never try to learn how to paint on large panels.

so paint a few parts and then read this paragraph again. The process will become more clear with practice.

I have also found that when I'm painting small parts it's best to hang them on a hook. You then flip the parts between the first and second coats. If you don't flip the parts between coats, you usually end up with thin or barren spots on the bottom edges.

One of the tricks of painting is to learn how to keep the wait time between coats to a minimum. Every paint is different. Some require a few seconds and others can take up to 15 minutes. The less time taken in the painting process leads to less dust and contaminants in the paint. If your wait time is too short, though, you will have runs and sags. It's a magic day when you figure out the formula, but I'm afraid you have to learn this the old-fashioned way – trial and error.

In an effort to save time, beginner painters attempt to paint several parts and panels all at once. The problem with this is that today's urethanes dry fairly quickly and over-spray gets on all of the parts. In order to compensate, the beginner then applies even more paint to keep the parts wet. Then all of the parts acquire runs in their paint and many choice words are spoken. It then takes three days to sand off the runs and the painter starts all over again. Even as a professional, I never paint more than two large panels at once.

This body has been color sanded and is ready for compounding. Once polished, the body is ready to be lowered onto the frame.

You will save yourself much misery if you start with small parts and then try no more than one door or fender. Once you feel comfortable with this, try a hood or trunk lid and finally graduate to the body section itself.

A nice, glossy paint job is not the final step in beautiful paint work. You must let the paint dry thoroughly, color sand the surface and buff out the paint. The drying time will vary between manufacturers, but I usually begin the compounding process on the second day after paint application. You will see that the surface will be wavy with an occasional peak or high spot. The first is called orange peel and is an unfortunate side effect to all standard and urethane enamel paints. The second is small dust or lint that lands and dries on the surfaces while painting. Painters call this "trash" and it's hard to prevent even with the most expensive booth. The remedy for these problems is color sanding.

Color sanding is merely a fancy term for wet sanding, and is a process where orange peel and defects are removed from the final coat of paint. Because urethane is relatively soft, it requires a different approach than lacquer. With urethanes, you should start with 1000- or 1500-grit wet sandpaper and move up to 2000 from there.

Polishing paint is not my favorite phase of auto restoration. It took me several months of hard work to learn how to polish well. The problem is that all of the flaws show up once the body has been buffed. There is a high risk of polishing through as well. Try not to get too discouraged if you find that you need more paint or worse, more body work!

There exist three basic sanding techniques. The first requires the use of a six-inch wet sanding block. This block should be used on all of the flat panels of the body. The second technique uses a 3M soft foam block. This is the same soft hand pad that I described in Chapter 13 for sanding curvy areas. Once again, this block is used to sand orange peel on those same areas. Finally, there will be situations where you will have to hold the sandpaper with your hand because nothing else will fit.

Generally, the sanding technique is similar to paint application in that a little sanding is applied at a time. It is important that only the minimum amount of paint is removed to eliminate orange peel and trash. Your paint supplier will sell little 3M squeegees. Sand a few strokes, and then squeegee the surface dry. In a few seconds, the remaining moisture will evaporate and you will see your progress. Only sand a little at a time and keep the surface flooded with water. This is done to allow any trash or contaminant to be removed from the sanded surface. If this is not done frequently, your sanding paper will trap some contaminant and grind deep scratches into the surface. You will not know that this has occurred until you are in the polishing phase.

While you are sanding, notice that the low spots of the orange peel will be shiny and several sanding strokes will be needed to thoroughly remove them. Also notice that the individual pieces of trash will be surrounded by shiny rings. Continue sanding until the entire panel is dull and free of flaws.

Occasionally you will sand the trash flush and still be able to see a discoloration or dark spot. This only happens with large trash and a judgment call has to be made as to whether or not the panel has to be repainted. If you are finished sanding and you see primer, you have to repaint the panel. This time you might want to add one more coat. Experience will tell you how many coats are actually needed for your brand of paint. I can tell you that if you are sanding through a fender with one quart of paint on it, then you are doing something wrong. Retrace your steps and find out why you are sanding off so much paint. More than likely, you are not applying the paint wet or smooth enough.

After you have finished sanding with 1500 grit, lightly hand sand the panel with 2000 grit. You are now ready for compounding. It is necessary to ask your paint supplier to recommend the proper buffing procedure for your brand of paint, but I have a general formula you can follow. I use a wool pad with a 3M non-abrasive urethane compound (Perfect-It II). The compound is applied to the pad and then rubbed on the paint at approximately 1500 rpm with an electric grinder/buffer. It is at this stage that all of the scratches and flaws should be rubbed out. The surface should be glossy with only small spider web scratches visible. Spider webbing is caused by small circular scratches and is usually the most visible in direct sunlight. Most cars I see have this problem. Once the compounding process is completed, change your pad to a 3M foam waffle pad and use 3M foam polishing compound at 1500 rpm to eliminate spider web scratches. At this point, you should be able to clearly read a newspaper's reflection in the side of your car – providing, of course, that you can read backwards!

When you are buffing paint, be conscious of the direction the pad is turning. Most machines rotate in a clockwise fashion. Never let the pad buff into an edge. Always slightly lift the machine so the pad pushes off an edge on the car. If the pad is allowed to buff directly into an edge, the paint will almost certainly buff through to the primer. This happens so fast that you usually see primer before you realize what you did. There might be some crevices that are so deep that the machine cannot be used. This situation is rare, but you can

The final result can be well worth the wait. Notice the image of the trees and sky along the side of the car. Now that's a car that will turn some heads!

polish urethane by hand with some compound, cheese cloth and time.

I do not want to downplay how difficult this is to do. I once painted a car in which the surface was not adequate for the customer. I then re-compounded the surface and broke through to the primer. Now aware of even finer detail and flaws, I repainted the car and tried again. I had to repeat this process for three long months before I really got good at polishing urethane paint. It can be an exasperating experience. There were a few times I almost broke down in tears due to frustration. Do not expect too much the first time you do this and *never* try to learn on large panels. Doors are perhaps the easiest to polish. Practice on them before anything else. Most of all, be patient and the skills will come in time.

Chapter 16

Body Assembly

Body by Fisher Service News is an example of existing literature that can aid in the reassembly of your car. Literature dealers that offer this type of resource can be found at the major swap meets across the country or in *Old Cars Weekly News & Marketplace* and *Hemmings Motor News*.

Body assembly can be rather complicated. It would not be practical to describe every single piece of the car. If I were to do so, this book would be thousands of pages long. I realize that most of you are looking for an assembly manual. I'm sad to report that most of you will never find one. There are reproduction manuals available for some General Motors late-1960s and early-1970s cars, but that's about it. However, all is not lost.

If you paid close attention at the beginning of this book you will already have an assembly manual. This is why you document everything you disassemble. Several years have probably passed since you were in the disassembly phase, but you should have a small book of notes that will now be priceless. Maybe you have noticed that the photos you took aren't very helpful. I have found this to be true as well. Photos just do not seem to show enough detail to be helpful. They are just there to document your work.

In addition to your journal, there are other resources you should know about. Make it a point to attend major swap meets. There are several people dealing in automotive literature who can be found at these shows. Remember that when a new car is produced, the manufacturer has to print literature to train and update the mechanics at the dealerships. This has been going on for decades. Literature dealers have everything from commercials to service news reports. Seek out the service news pamphlets that pertain to your car's marque and year. These pamphlets cost around $25 and can be worth their weight in gold. If you have difficulty finding information in your marque or year, remember that several marques within a company can be similar. For example, Pontiacs and Chevrolets are cousins to each other. You will also notice similarities in back-to-back years such as 1951-'52, 1953-'54, 1955-'56, etc.

There is one piece of information about auto assembly that took me several years to really understand. One measurement of a finely restored automobile is the gaps, or spaces between the panels. You have probably seen the television commercial where a ball bearing is placed in the gaps of a car and then allowed to roll around the seams as the car is turned in a huge rotisserie. It wasn't an effective commercial because the average consumer didn't have a clue what that meant. Judges like to see straight and uniform seams on a car. For instance, the space between the rear door edge and the door jam should be the same width all the way down the door. This is what is referred to as a gap. You have gaps between the doors and fenders, fenders and hood and around the trunk lid. All of these gaps should be approximately three-sixteenths of an inch wide. You achieve correct gaps through panel adjustment and the use of shims.

The first gaps you will encounter are around the doors. You will notice that the doors can be adjusted in several ways. Attach the door to the door hinge and slowly close the door. Be careful, because the door could be so far out of adjustment that it will scrape the finished paint around the jam. Try to get the door as parallel to the rocker panel as pos-

The doors are the first panels that have to be aligned. Proper panel alignment will help set your car apart from the rest.

Notice that the bottom edge of the door is parallel to the rocker panel. This is accomplished with the adjustments at the leading door edge and at the hinge itself. The trailing door edge is aligned by placing shims on the car frame at either the front and back, or at the middle. These shims slightly bend the car body to get proper door gaps.

When you are adjusting the doors, a friend can help keep the door steady while you make your door adjustments. Remember that you will have to repeat this process several times before you get it right. Air ratchets are useful here.

sible. This is done with the adjustment at the hinge. Sometimes the hinge has to be adjusted, too. This is necessary when you close the door and notice that its bottom edge will not get flush with the rocker panel. This whole process can take a day or more with just one door, so be patient. Most of the time, you will get the door parallel to the rocker and the gap between the door and the quarter panel just will not get straight. This is fixed by adding shims between the frame and body mounts. More than likely, you saw (and hopefully saved) several such shims during the disassembly phase. If the gap at the top of the door is tight, add shims to the center of the frame. If the gap at the top of the door is too large, add shims to the front and rear of the frame. This actually bends the car body to the correct shape.

The next panel to be installed is the trunk lid. Trunk lid installation has aggravated car enthusiasts for years, but I have discovered a trick. You can usually get the trunk lid straight with uniform gaps all the way around, but it seems that it's

always troublesome to align the front gap or the gap located between the lid and the deck. What usually happens is the lid will not get flush with the deck. In other words, the trunk lid will be either too high or too low. Once again, this is fixed with shims. Experiment by placing shims where the trunk lid bolts to its hinges. There are usually four bolts (two per side) that hold the lid in place. Placing a shim at one of these bolt locations radically changes the pitch of the lid. It doesn't take long to find the right combination. Incidentally, most car manufacturers painted their cars with the doors and trunk lids installed, so these bolts should be body color.

The insulation inside the trunk lid can sometimes be purchased, but those of you with older cars will have to resort to an old trick. Find a parts car sedan and remove the headliner. You will find that the manufacturer used the same insulation on the roof. Use a heating torch on the top of the roof. This will loosen the glue that holds the insulation in place. Once removed, it can be cut into the appropriate sizes to fit into the trunk lid holes. This technique takes a little practice so start with just one hole at a time. This trick gives the insulation a "like new" appearance. The perimeter of this

Always recruit help when installing large, heavy pieces. Notice that all hands are positioned between the trunk lid and the body of the car. This is done to protect both panels if the lid should slip.

The procedure begins to get repetitive and easier with practice. Notice that the air hose is draped over the back of the person at left. Once again, this is done to protect the car's finish.

insulation should be painted body color to mimic the original appearance.

After the trunk lid, you will find that the hood is fairly straightforward. If you have any problems with the hood alignment, the hood hinges are almost always the culprit. The fenders shouldn't be any harder, but sometimes you find that additional door hinge adjustments are needed to get the fenders to line up flush with the doors. Once the fenders are installed, lower the hood slowly. You usually find that additional hood adjustments are needed as well. This whole process takes weeks, so be patient. Panel alignment can be one of the most tedious phases in auto restoration – right up there with block sanding!

Keep in mind that I have shimmed thousands of parts. Through this whole process, you have to have the dash assembled, chrome plating done, stainless trim polished, engine compartment finished, upholstery done, etc. The list goes on and on.

Upholstery is not that difficult. You can usually find someone in your state that does good work. Always get a reference beforehand from a car enthusiast at a show. *Old*

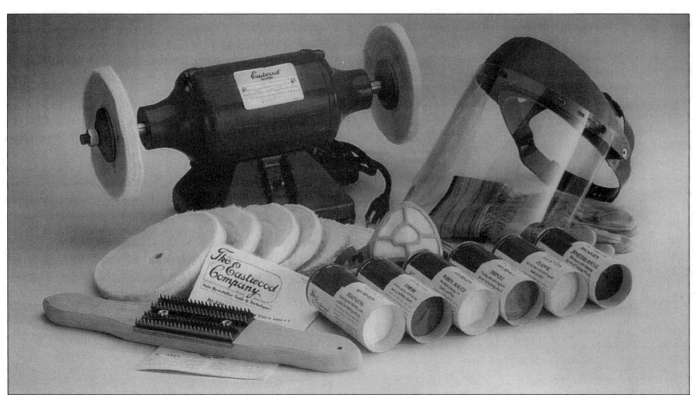

The Eastwood Company offers a nice stainless kit that has several uses. (Photos courtesy of The Eastwood Company)

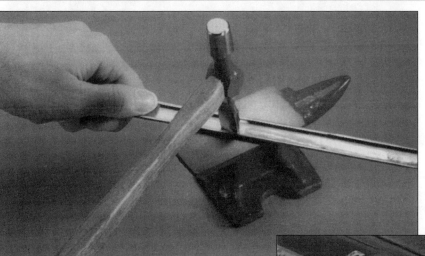

You would be amazed what can be done with old plastic parts. The plastic polishing system can make taillights look like new again. Unfortunately, there are some limitations. Once the plastic has crazed or cracked, there is little that can be done to save it. (Photo courtesy of The Eastwood Company)

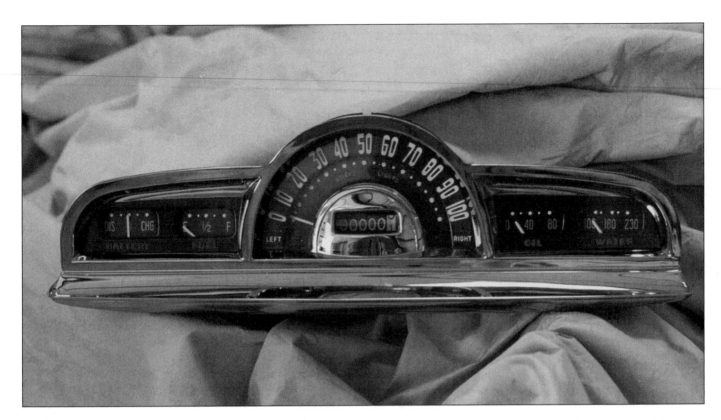

NOS instruments are useful. New gauges, chrome and a buffed plastic lens can give the driver the illusion that he has stepped back in time.

Cars Weekly News & Marketplace or *Hemmings Motor News* can be sources for locating chrome platers. I use Faith Plating and J&P Plating. I had trouble finding a good source for stainless trim polishing, so I decided to teach myself how to do it. There are several training videos that can help you with this. If you have a part that is mangled or severely dented, try to find a replacement piece through your club or in *Old Cars Weekly News & Marketplace* or *Hemmings Motor News*.

Do not let yourself become caught up in acquiring new old stock (NOS) parts. There are several dealers who distribute NOS parts, but you don't need that many. Various plastic trim pieces will be needed and NOS dash instruments come in handy as well. Some plastic parts will be impossible to find. Contact EmbleMagic. They can manufacture just about any plastic emblem you need. Most of the rubber parts can be obtained from companies advertising in *Old Cars Weekly News & Marketplace* or *Hemmings Motor News* as well. There will be instances where rubber parts are just not available. This usually happens with rare or off-marque cars. The only way to handle this is to search for the piece you need on parts cars. Sooner or later you will find a good piece, and it can be restored with a little silicone spray and elbow grease.

New wiring harnesses can also be found in *Old Cars Weekly News & Marketplace* or *Hemmings Motor News.* I've always used Y-N-Zs in California as my harness source. Most glass pieces can be found in *Old Cars Weekly News & Marketplace* or

Hemmings Motor News as well. You see *Old Cars Weekly News & Marketplace* and *Hemmings Motor News* a lot in this paragraph. Get these publications and read them. You will have to rely on your club and your instincts the rest of the way. As you can tell, this chapter could be endless. Take your time and *never* place large deposits with anyone in this business. There are numerous people in the hobby that make their living just from deposits. I use several-year-old copies of *Old Cars Weekly News & Marketplace* or *Hemmings Motor News* to locate reputable companies. I figure that if the companies are still around after several years, they must be legitimate. Good luck and be cautious with your trust!

A new wire harness is a necessity. There is just no practical way to restore or install the old harness.

Chapter 17

Proper Care

If you need more garage space, Cover-It offers all kinds of affordable garages.

Once your long restoration journey has come to an end, how do you take care of your pride and joy? The most important tip I could give you would be to stay out of the sunlight. I'm not suggesting that you never take the car out for a spin or to a show. A car is a machine and it should be enjoyed. However, it is important to store the car in a garage. The obvious benefit is protection from the elements, but it also provides security. There has been an increase in the theft of classic automobiles. If you store it outside, you are just asking for trouble. I know of a guy in Texas who was trying to sell his late-1960s muscle car. He placed ads in the newspaper and parked the car on the side of the road for viewing. In a few days, the car was gone, and I don't mean from a sale!

I strongly recommend purchasing an enclosed trailer for those of you with frame-off restorations. I know they are not cheap, but think of all the money and time you have invested in your car. I cannot tell you how many people have $50,000 and six years invested in a car, head out for their first show and are hailed on! Even if it rains, and it probably will, do you have any idea how long it takes to clean a car from top to bottom and underneath?

I was at a car show in Illinois a few years back. Everything was going well. The day before the show and shine everyone was outside with their buckets of water washing their cars. The weather was beautiful, but all of a sudden the temperature began to drop. We looked out on the horizon and a large front was approaching. Now this was no ordinary front. The clouds were black and green. I have only seen clouds this ugly once before, and they were followed by a tornado and hailstorm. Naturally, people began to panic. No problem for those of us who had enclosed trailers; we just started up our cars and drove into our portable garages. Fortunately there were no tornadoes or hail that day, but I hope you get the point. I'm not suggesting that a trailer can stop a tornado, but it will protect your car from rain, hail, vandalism and even theft. If you decide to sell your car, never leave it unsupervised at the side of the road.

It would be a shame to spend several years restoring a beauty like this and then have some thief drive off in it. Never leave a car on the side of the road when it comes time to sell.

Here's a neat space saver. The Eastwood Company offers these small dollies. Once all four tires are on dollies, the car can be moved in any direction by just one person. (Photo courtesy of The Eastwood Company)

There is one myth about cars that I hope I shattered in Chapter 15, that being more coats of paint result in a better paint job. Well, there is one more myth to debunk. This is the one you probably learned from your father or saw in the "Karate Kid" movie. Everybody seems to wax or clean their cars in circular motions. The next time you see a fairly new car, look at it in direct sunlight. Those swirl, spider web-like scratches were not installed at the factory. The owner put those there! To avoid this, always wipe the car in straight lines down the length of the car. This will still put the same microscopic scratches on the surface, but straight scratches do not reflect light as do the circular ones. This means no spider webs.

In addition, I never wash my car. I use a product called Dri Wash-N-Guard. When I'm not using my car, I keep it indoors and covered with a car cover. This minimizes dust buildup. Before I take it out, all I have to do is dust off the car with a California car duster from The Eastwood Company. After that, I spray on a light mist of Dri Wash and wipe it off in straight lines with an old cotton shirt. The whole process takes me less than 10 minutes. I cannot help chuckling every time during a show weekend when I see those guys with

Enclosed trailers cost between $8,000-$12,000. It sounds expensive, but ask yourself how much money and time you already have invested in your car. Enclosed trailers can be your best insurance policy against Mother Nature's wrath. (Photo courtesy of Bruce Litton Trailer Sales)

their buckets of soap waiting in line for the hotel's only water hose.

Those of you that live in colder climates have a few more chores during the winter. Most people put their cars on blocks. The main reason for this is to protect the tires. If a car sits in one place for a long time, the tires have a tendency to crack at the bottom. This problem is intensified in colder climates. It is a good idea to spray all of the rubber on the car with protectant as well. The nice thing about Dri Wash is that it can be used on paint, rubber, chrome and glass. It has greatly simplified car shows for me. I no longer have to haul a box of cleaning chemicals around. Try it and judge for yourself.

 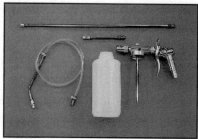

For those of you not interested in owning frame-off show cars, you might want to consider undercoating your car for rust protection. The Eastwood Company offers a handy and affordable undercoating kit. (Photo courtesy of The Eastwood Company)

Chapter 18

Thou Shalt Not Worship False Gods

From time-to-time I run across people who cannot be made happy. No matter how perfect their car is, they are not satisfied. No human being is perfect, and that includes you. It is easy to become obsessed with a restoration. The problem is that there are different levels of flaws. Once you have been successful in eliminating flaws at a certain level, a whole new set of flaws become visible. Somehow they are not noticed when compared to the other, more visible ones. Guess what? You can spend months fixing these newfound flaws and come up with a whole new list the next day. Sometimes a flaw can't be located until one is fixed (for example, wavy body work won't be detected if the paint's finish is dull). Trust me, it never ends. The people who are caught up in this usually end up bitter and disappointed.

You will also meet critics at car shows. These are the people love to go from car-to-car and tell the owners what is wrong with their dream cars. What irks me is that most of these people do not even have a car at the show. No matter how tempting it is to confront these pests (or pepper spray them!), don't do it. That's the reaction they're waiting for. They are miserable people who will not be happy until you are miserable, too.

I've enjoyed writing this book and I hope it helps steer you away from the pitfalls of automotive restoration. Good luck and God bless.

Appendix

Painting defects recognition, prevention, corrections

(Photos and information courtesy of Spies Hecker Inc.)

Despite careful preparation, modern application technology and the use of sophisticated paint systems, defects can never be completely ruled out in vehicle refinishing. However, a professional body shop today cannot afford to produce bad-quality results. And repairing a defect often takes a great deal of time and effort.

What are the causes, what mistakes were made? Spies Hecker has compiled the most frequent defects a painter encounters into this easy-to-use reference.

It is only when a defect has been correctly identified can causes be eliminated and the damage to the painted object efficiently repaired.

The examples and solutions given here will enable painting defects to be prevented, thereby guaranteeing top-quality results.

> **All paint companies have technical assistance available. If any of the flaws on the following pages show up in your paint work, contact your local paint supplier. A representative will be sent to help you.**

Dirt and dust

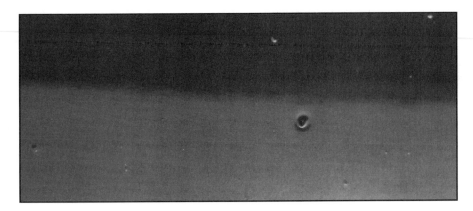

Definition

- Particles protruding from the surface of the coat.

Cause

- The vehicle surface was not effectively cleaned before paint application.
- The air filters need replacing.
- The pressure in the spray booth was too low.
- The painters were wearing unsuitable clothing.

Prevention

- Before painting ensure the vehicle surface has been properly cleaned with a tack cloth.
- Check the filters regularly.
- Wear overalls that are free of lint.
- Make sure the spray booth is maintained in a clean condition.

Remedy

- Lightly sand and polish the affected area.
- If this is unsuccessful, sand the entire area, clean with silicone remover and respray.

Stains (metallics)

Definition

- Discolored patches on metallic top coats (such as blotch at left in photo).

Cause

- Areas of primer surfacer or putty were sanded.
- Too much hardener was used in polyester putty.

Prevention

- Apply a sealer coat on the sanded-through areas.
- Avoid too much hardener in polyester putty.

Remedy

- Sand the entire area when it has dried through, clean with silicone remover and re-spray.
- If too much hardener was used in polyester putty, seal with spray polyester and re-apply the paint system.

Runs or sags

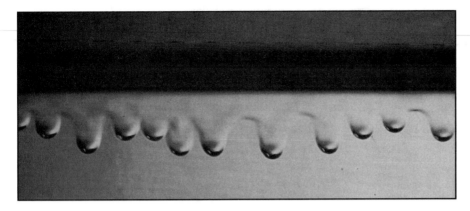

Definition

- Paint runs on vertical body parts.

Cause

- Uneven paint application.
- The spraying viscosity was incorrect.
- Unsuitable thinners were used.
- Air, material or ambient temperature was too low.
- Film thicknesses were too high.
- Defective spray gun (nozzle).
- Intermediate flash-off time was too short.

Prevention

- Warm object and paint up to room temperature of 20 degrees C / 68 degrees F.
- Ensure that the spray gun is in good working order. Follow application recommendations in technical data sheets.

Remedy

- After the paint has hardened thoroughly, sand the runs flat, lightly sand the entire area, if necessary allow to dry, clean with silicone remover and respray.
- With smaller defects, polish the affected area after sanding.

Pores / Pin holes

Definition

- Pin-prick sized holes as deep as the surfacer coat.

Cause

- Excessive film thicknesses in conjunction with forced drying.
- Pores in the putty surface were not filled.

Prevention

- Apply surfacer at normal film thicknesses.
- Keep to the recommended flash-off times.

Remedy

- Allow top coat to dry through, then sand affected areas, clean with silicone remover, seal with a two-pack primer surfacer and respray.
- In severe cases sand down the top coat completely and reapply the entire paint system.

Solvent Popping

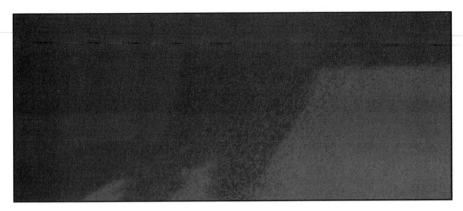

Definition

- Small bubbles and pop marks in the top coat.

Cause

- Paint was applied at excessive film thicknesses.
- Top coat was not allowed to flash off long enough before low baking.
- Spray viscosity was not correct.
- Unsuitable hardener or reducer was used.

Prevention

- Apply normal film thicknesses.
- Keep to correct flash-off times.
- Use spray viscosity, hardeners and reducers given in the technical data sheet.

Remedy

- Allow to dry through, then sand the affected areas, clean with silicone remover, seal any fine pores with two-pack acrylic primer surfacer and respray.
- Where popping is more extensive, sand down top coat completely and reapply paint system.

Cratering / Fish-eyes

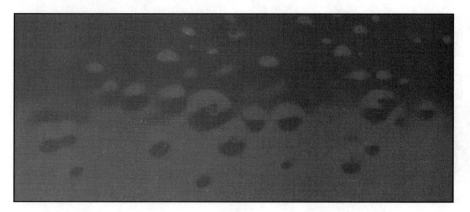

Definition

- Crater-like depressions with raised edges.

Cause

- Substrate was not thoroughly cleaned with silicone remover.

- Air supply was contaminated with oil or water.

- Ceiling filter does not meet the requirements.

Prevention

- Check that regular maintenance is carried out on the air lines.

- Ensure that the filter is changed regularly (secondary filter about once a year, primary filter every three months).

- Clean surfaces properly with silicone remover before repairing and refinishing.

Remedy

- Sand, clean with silicone remover and reapply top coat.

Edge mapping

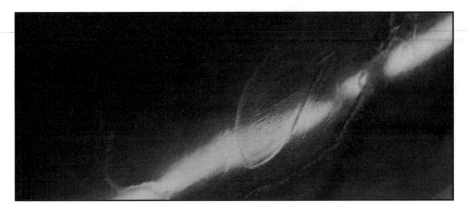

Definition

- Ringing in the top coat around repairs.

Cause

- Sanded area not smoothly blended into old finish.
- Putty and surfacer were applied on top of elastic factory finishes.
- Surfacer was not allowed to dry through before being sanded and recoated.
- The substrate was not fully cured.
- Preparatory material applied at excessive film thicknesses and not allowed to dry properly.

Prevention

- Carry out a solvent test on the exposed paint layers (elastic/hard).
- Only apply putty on bare metal.
- With elastic factory finishes, apply surfacer to the entire area.

Remedy

- After the top coat has dried thoroughly, sand and polish damaged area, if necessary seal with primer surfacer, and respray.

Pores in surfacer coat

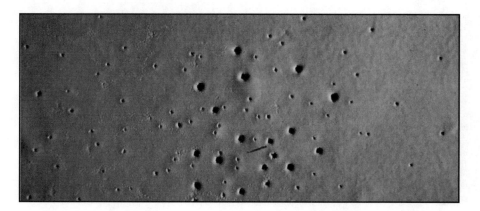

Definition

- Small, pin-hole like depressions.

Cause

- Spray viscosity was too high.
- Unsuitable hardener was used, ea. fast hardener at high temperatures.
- Excessive film thicknesses.

Prevention

- Follow the application recommendations in the technical data sheet.
- Choose the correct hardener for the ambient temperature.
- Apply surfacer at the recommended film thicknesses.

Remedy

- Sand down and reapply paint system.

Sanding marks

Definition

- Scratches with swollen edges.

Cause

- The abrasive paper used to sand the putty or surfacer was too coarse.
- The surfacer was not allowed to dry sufficiently before recoating.

Prevention

- Use the recommended abrasive paper for sanding: Putty: first sanding P 180, final sanding P 320. Surfacer: dry P 400, wet P 800.
- Follow instructions for drying the surfacer given in the technical data sheet.

Remedy

- When the top coat has dried through, finely sand and polish the affected area.
- For deeper marks, sand and reapply top coat.

Specks (metallics)

Definition

- Points protruding from the paint film.

Cause

- Metallic base coat was not applied wet enough for the metallic particles to settle into the paint.
- The clear coat was not able to cover these vertical particles.

Prevention

- Apply the base coat in accordance with the instructions in the technical data sheet.
- Maintain the correct distance between spray gun and object (approximately eight inches).

Remedy

- Allow clear coat to dry, lightly sand with P 800, clean with silicone remover and re-apply clear coat.

Solvent attack / Pick-up / Rippling

Definition

- Lifting/wrinkling of the paint surface.

Cause

- Substrate was not fully cured or is solvent-sensitive.

- Areas where clear coat was sanded through to base coat were not sealed with a suitable primer surfacer.

- Unsuitable substrate (TPA) and nitrocellulose paints.

- Unsuitable priming materials, top coats or reducers were used.

Prevention

- Carry out solvent test on problematic substrates.

- On difficult substrates apply several thin coats of two-pack primer surfacer and allow longer flash-off times.

Remedy

- Allow to dry through, completely remove both the wrinkled top coat and the contaminated substrate and reapply the paint system.

- Before applying the top coat, sand the entire area.

Blistering

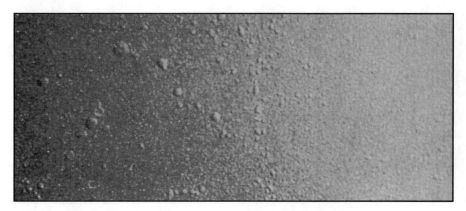

Definition

- Small raised dots in the surface.

Cause

- Moisture was absorbed by the substrate.

- Areas to be painted were not allowed to dry completely after wet sanding (particularly a problem with polyester products). Air humidity before painting was too high.

- Temperature fluctuation led to condensation.

- Pores/pin holes in the substrate were not sanded out.

- Polyester products were not sealed.

Prevention

- Only dry sand polyester products and apply sealer coat.

- Carefully sand out or apply more putty to fill pin holes.

- Check the air humidity regularly.

Remedy

- Sand down the affected area completely, sand the remaining surface well, clean with silicone remover, apply primer surfacer and then top coat.

Die back / Matting / Gloss

Definition

- Loss of gloss on the top coat.

Cause

- Surfacer was not allowed to dry sufficiently.
- Unsuitable reducers were used, causing the substrate to dissolve.
- Contaminated hardener was used.
- Excessive film build of top coat.

Prevention

- Keep to the drying times given in the technical data sheets.
- Use only the recommended reducers.
- Close hardener cans firmly after use to ensure proper seal.
- Apply top coat as per technical data sheets.

Remedy

- After drying, polish the affected area to remove the matting, or lightly sand the entire surface, clean with silicone remover and respray.

Cratering in the surfacer

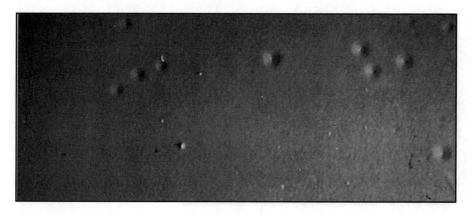

Definition

- Crater-like depressions with raised edges.

Cause

- Substrate was not sufficiently cleaned with silicone remover.

- Air supply contaminated with oil or water (defective oil and water separator in air line).

Prevention

- Thoroughly clean the substrate with silicone remover.

- Ensure that regular maintenance is carried out on the air lines.

Remedy

- Allow to dry and then sand out the cratering.

- Clean the entire area and reapply surfacer.

Water marks

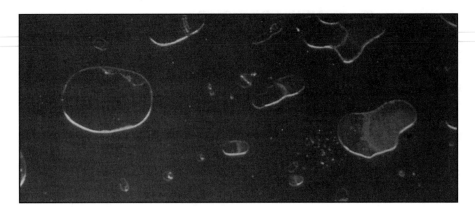

Definition

- Round marks on the paint surface.

Cause

- Water droplets evaporated off fresh paint work which is not fully dry; this is mainly a problem on horizontal surfaces.

Prevention

- Keep to the drying times given in the technical data sheets.

Remedy

- Where isolated marking has occurred, lightly sand with P 1000 and then polish.

- With severe contamination, sand the area well, clean with silicone remover and re-spray.

Orange peel

Definition

- Uneven surface formation resembling orange peel.

Cause

- Spray viscosity was too high.
- Fast reducers/hardeners were used.
- Temperature in the spray booth was too high.
- Distance between spray nozzle and object was too great, paint was applied too dry.

Prevention

- Set the spray booth temperature at approximately 20 degrees C / 68 degrees F.
- Use a suitable reducer hardener for the particular repair.
- Check the paint viscosity with a DIN viscosity cup.
- Maintain a spraying distance of approximately eight inches.

Remedy

- Sand down the uneven surface and respray.

Corrosion / Rusting

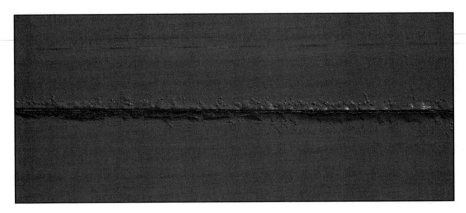

Definition

- Mechanical damage with rusting under the paint film.

Cause

- Stone chipping combined with road salt and moisture.
- Moisture on bare metal prior to priming.

Prevention

- Thoroughly clean and blow off bare metal prior to priming.

Remedy

- Sand paint down to the metal.
- Refinish with one-pack corrosion primer, then the usual surfacer and top coat.

Staining

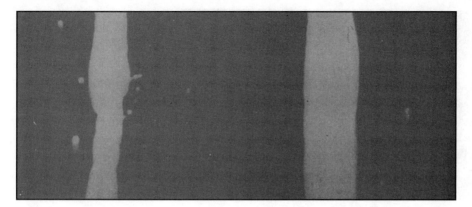

Definition

- Occasional stains on the finish.

Cause

- Contamination of the surface by chemically reactive materials such as chalk, cement dust, strong detergent cleaners and bird droppings.

Remedy

- In most cases gloss can be restored by polishing.

- If this is not successful, sand the area, clean with silicone remover and respray.

- If necessary, sand down and reapply the paint system.

Water blisters

Definition

- Medium-sized blisters in the top coat.

Cause

- Residues of sanding water which have collected in corners, edges and under moldings. Contaminated air supply.

Prevention

- Blow clean air into recesses after sanding to check they are dry. Always remove add-on parts if possible.

- Check regularly that oil and water separator on compressed air line is working efficiently.

Remedy

- For light contamination, sand damaged area and then polish.

- Where contamination is more severe, sand and respray.

Mottling / Striping

Definition

- Uneven color or special effect formation.

Cause

- Defective spray gun (nozzle).

- Fluctuating air pressure, unsuitable reducer, incorrect spraying technique, incorrect spraying viscosity.

Prevention

- Use mixing stick or DIN viscosity cup to set spraying viscosity. Ensure spray guns are maintained regularly. Keep spray gun parallel to object while spraying at a distance of approximately eight inches. Follow closely the application recommendations in the technical data sheets.

Remedy

- Allow to dry thoroughly then sand surface and respray with top coat system.

Peeling problems with polyester material

Definition

- Areas of polyester putty peeling off.

Cause

- Substrate was not carefully prepared.
- Unsuitable polyester putty was used.
- Infra-red drying was not carried out correctly.

Prevention

- The substrate must be cleaned and sanded thoroughly. Before applying polyester putty, carefully read the technical data sheet.
- Use putties and primers that are recommended for galvanized substrates.
- Follow the manufacturer's instructions for infra-red drying.

Remedy

- Sand the defective paint work well, then repair and refinish with suitable materials.

Low hiding power / Opacity

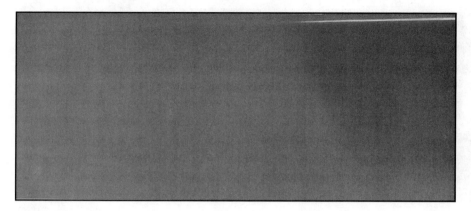

Definition

• Uneven color of finish.

Cause

• Wrong surfacer used for three-stage systems. Insufficient application of top coat.

Prevention

• Ensure top coats are applied at recommended film thicknesses. With low opacity colors, use the surfacer stipulated. Apply a neutral-colored primer surfacer.

Remedy

• Sand and respray.

Polishing marks

Definition

- Round polishing marks of various sizes with reduced gloss or an uneven surface that was polished through.

Cause

- Unsuitable polishing compound was used. The surface was uneven, leading to high spots being polished through. Polishing was carried out before the top coat was dried through.

Prevention

- Use suitable polishing compounds and equipment. Check that the top coat is completely dry before polishing.

Remedy

- Ensure that the top coat is completely dry and then repolish. If affected areas are still visible, sand and respray.

Supplier Listing

Bill Hirsh Auto Parts
396 Littleton Ave.
Newark, NJ 07103
(201)642-2404

Bruce Litton Trailer Sales
P.O. Box 34174
Indianapolis, IN 46234
(317)293-7007

Classic Exhaust (stainless steel)
182 Industrial Parkway
Cleveland, GA 30528
(706)865-5433

Classic & Performance Specialties
(stainless steel brake/fuel lines)
80 Rotech Dr.
Lancaster, NY 14086
1(800)882-3711

Cover-It Instant Garages
17 Wood St.
West Haven, CT 06516-3843
1(800)932-9344
web site: www.cover-it-inc.com

Dri-Wash
P.O. Box 1331
Palm Desert, CA 92261
1(800)428-1883

EmbleMagic
8367 Shepard Rd.
Macedonia, OH 44056
(216)467-8755

Egge Machine Co.
11707 Slauson Ave.
Sante Fe Springs, CA 90670
(310)945-3419

Evercoat Fibreglass
6600 Cornell Rd.
Cincinnati, OH 45242
1(800)729-7600

Faith Plating
7141 Santa Monica Blvd.
Los Angeles, CA 90046
(213)851-0100

Hemmings Motor News
P.O. Box 100
Bennington, VT 05201
(802)447-9550

Henderson Automotive
2457 S. Loop 4, Bldg. 5A
Buda, TX 78610
(512)295-4295

J & P Plating
807 N. Meridian St.
Portland, IN 47371
(219)726-9696

Kanter Auto Products
76 Monroe St.
Boonton, NJ 07005
1(800)526-1096

Old Cars Weekly News & Marketplace
    700 E. State St.
    Iola, WI 54990
    1(800)258-0929
    web site: www.krause.com

Restoration Specialties and Supply Inc.
    P.O. Box 328
    Windber, PA 15963
    (814)467-9282

Roto-Body-Frame
    6 Taunya Lane
    Travelers Rest, SC 29690
    (864)834-9209

Spies Hecker Inc.
    55 Sea Lane
    Farmingdale, NY 11735
    (516)777-7100

Steele Rubber Products Inc.
    6180 Hwy 150 E
    Denver, NC 28037
    1(800)544-8665

Suburban Auto Upholstery
    1 SW Fifth St.
    Lee's Summit, MO 64063
    (816)246-6321

The Eastwood Company
    580 Lancaster Ave.
    Malvern, PA 19355-0714
    1(800)345-1178
    web site: www.eastwoodco.com

TIP Tools and Equipment (Truman's Inc.)
    P.O. Box 649
    Canfield, OH 44406
    1(800)321-9260
    web site: www.tiptools.com

White Post Restorations
    One Old Car Dr.
    White Post, VA 22663
    (540)837-1140

YnZ's Yesterdays Parts (wiring harnesses)
    333 E. Stuart Ave.
    Redlands, CA 92374
    (909)798-1498